"Katie Arnold, a runner and a writer, does not turn back but turns toward and then turns inward in this miraculous and beautiful book about awakening. Her luminous writing sheds light on a life that is true and revelatory. This book is a must read for all of us on how to meet life fully and bravely."

—JOAN HALIFAX, author of *Standing at the Edge*

"This is a wise, vivid book about acceptance and forgiveness, about pushing to our outer limits, both body and soul, in order to find a new kind of wonder, love, and grace."

—MICHAEL PATERNITI, author of *Driving Mr. Albert*

"*Brief Flashings in the Phenomenal World* wrestles with a paradox as slippery as wet river rock: If you want to find yourself, start by becoming utterly lost. Author and runner Katie Arnold did just that, and she returns to us now with this honest, lyrical, and exuberant book. The peace she's found radiates through these pages."

—CHRISTOPHER SOLOMON, *Outside* and *Runner's World* magazines

"A spellbinding narrative delivering wise and unassuming insights on what it means to be a runner, a mother, a spouse and a reluctant fan of the eighties-era pop star Eddie Money. When she writes of the 'dazzling, peculiar alchemy' embodied by cliff divers plummeting to the sea, she could well be describing the restrained and supple grace that pervades this beautiful book."

—BILL DONAHUE, author of *Unbound: Unforgettable True Stories from the World of Endurance Sports*

"Katie Arnold has a deep wisdom about the ground of being. She understands it through her body, through running, and the natural world. She doesn't just write about it, she transmits it. This book is a beautiful exploration of what it means to be truly alive."

—NATALIE GOLDBERG, author of *Three Simple Lines*

"This wise, lyrical book unfolds like a koan: How can a devastating accident on a river help you become the river? Katie Arnold shows us how humility, curiosity, and courage can open us to the beauty and wild energy of the world."

—FLORENCE WILLIAMS, author of *Heartbreak: A Personal and Scientific Journey*

"Only a writer of prodigious insight and blazing talent could create a book like *Brief Flashings in the Phenomenal World*, which is at once a spiritual guide, a grand adventure, a writing manual, and a story told from the heart that grips other hearts and tells them, 'slow down. Look around. It is *all* phenomenal.'"

—TRACY ROSS, author of *The Source of All Things*

"Part memoir and part meditation, *Brief Flashings in the Phenomenal World* meanders through midlife troubles both extraordinary and mundane—from a dramatic rafting injury to simmering tensions that threaten a marriage—as Arnold turns to Zen to find ways to cope. In narrative streams that mirror the currents and eddies of the rivers she loves, Arnold offers a quietly joyous testament to the beauty of imperfection and the power of learning to flow, fully and freely, within one's own life."

—MARIN SARDY, author of *The Edge of Everyday*

"Katie Arnold writes like a dream. A wild philosophical ride through the hard rapids of adulthood—marriage, rivers, running, children, the natural world, and more. Plus, this is definitely one of the rowdiest books on Zen ever written."

—STEVEN KOTLER, author of *The Rise of Superman*

"Katie Arnold's descriptions of running, whether through glorious mountains or bitter weather, whether in beautiful flow states or grueling agonies that call forth spectacular perseverance, make for electrifying and irresistible reading. I can't get enough of them."

—HENRY SHUKMAN, author of *One Blade of Grass*

"Runner and writer Katie Arnold has written a deeply thoughtful, lyrical book on the frailties not just of the human body but of the human heart. Marrying Zen tenets with day-to-day disappointments, sudden wonders, and the obligations, both banal and joyous, that come with being wife, mother, lover of the outdoors, and citizen of the world, Arnold offers wise insights for all of us on this long ultramarathon called Life."

—CAROLINE PAUL, author of *Tough Broad*

"*Brief Flashings in the Phenomenal World* is a gorgeous and moving meditation on the never-straight, never-simple, riverlike journey of Zen."

—HARLEY RUSTAD, author of *Lost in the Valley of Death*

BRIEF
FLASHINGS

in the

PHENOMENAL
WORLD

Zen and
the Art of
Running Free

KATIE ARNOLD

PARALLAX PRESS
BERKELEY, CALIFORNIA

Parallax Press
2236 Sixth Street, Suite B
Berkeley, CA 94710
parallax.org

Parallax Press is the publishing division of Plum Village Community
of Engaged Buddhism
© 2024 Katie Arnold

Cover design by Katie Eberle
Interior design by Maureen Forys, Happenstance Type-O-Rama
Author photograph © Owen Lipstein
Original cover photograph by Jack Brauer

Shunryu Suzuki's work and excerpts from *Zen Mind, Beginner's Mind,* pro-
tected under the terms of the International Copyright Union, have been
reprinted by arrangement with The Permissions Company, LLC on behalf
of Shambhala Publications Inc., Boulder, Colorado, shambhala.com.

Printed in Canada by Friesens
Printed on 100 percent recycled paper

Library of Congress Control Number: 2023949114
ISBN: 978-1-952692-69-7

1 2 3 4 5   FRIESENS   28 27 26 25 24

CONTENTS

FOR STEVE

*"When you realize that everything is just a
flashing into the vast universe, you become very strong
and your existence becomes very meaningful."*

—SHUNRYU SUZUKI

*"No, I'd never been to this country before.
No, I didn't know where the roads would lead me.
No, I didn't intend to turn back."*

—MARY OLIVER

How do you tell a story that's beyond words? The question is its own kind of Zen koan—you won't find the answer by thinking but by living. It might take years to solve. You must be willing to let go of everything you know. You will have to stop looking in order to find it. It can't be told in the usual way, with three acts and an epiphany. The mind, like time, isn't linear. It jumps from now to then and back again. It bends and braids like a river, rising and falling in the shape of mountains, in the space of a breath. It comes and goes in waves, doubling back on itself like the lip of a rapid or the folded fortune tellers my daughters make out of paper. *Pick a number*, they tell me. Our stories are built from bits and pieces, broken fragments we string together, determined by chance and choice, accident and intent—sudden bursts of understanding that illuminate the truth of who we are. You write your story with your body; read it this way, too. There are a dozen different outcomes, no one beginning or end. Every possibility already exists.

INTRODUCTION

On a cold, snowy December evening just after Christmas in 2018, I drove half a mile from my house to a Zen Buddhist temple at the foot of a small mountain in Santa Fe. It was not long past sunset, but the dirt road was dark, and the only light was my headlights, two bright cones illuminating the flashing blizzard and the narrow, quickly-filling tracks of a car that had traveled the road just ahead of me.

I was going to give a talk about running and Zen. I was so nervous I felt like throwing up. Also, I was strangely calm. It was the darkest night in the darkest month of year and the snow fell softly and with great determination and steadiness. The effect was transfixing, as though I was riding a night train to adventure in deepest, farthest Siberia. Something mysterious lay ahead. I was going to discover what it was.

At first, giving a talk had seemed like a wonderful idea. I'd learned about Zen through running and about running through Zen and about life through both, and I hoped I might have something to offer that could be of use to someone somewhere, fumbling through the dark mysteries of their own life.

As the date approached, however, I began to worry. I'm not exactly a walking advertisement for Zen. I wear bright colors, and I move fast. I can run thirty miles, but when I meditate, the longest I seem to manage is fifteen minutes, twenty-five if I'm feeling very strong. What did I know about sitting! Running was my practice.

I realized that I would have to say something that made sense and contributed to the greater good, in front of a room full of people who had probably been studying Zen for far longer than I, and much more dutifully, and I fell into a mild panic. I'd been absorbing the ideas of Zen and Buddhism by osmosis for a decade, but suddenly everything I thought I understood was slipping like seaweed through my grasp. I needed to get a handle on the basics. I needed an explanation.

I went to see my friend Natalie. She'd been practicing Zen for more than thirty years. She would know. "What *is* Zen?" I asked her desperately.

When Natalie and I met almost a decade earlier, we hiked up the mountain above the Zen center every week. It was winter, and some mornings the thermometer barely edged above twenty degrees. The trail was snowy and slick with ice in the shady patches. My father had just died, and my grief tricked me into believing I was dying, too. I carried my five-month-old daughter, Maisy, in a pack on my chest. Walking up the mountain with Natalie was an act of survival: it meant I was still alive, that maybe I wouldn't die that day, or the next. On the most frigid of mornings, the landline in our kitchen would ring during breakfast and I knew even before answering that it was Natalie, calling to ask, "Should we go?" And I always said yes. Whatever the weather, we went.

Natalie was in her late sixties with clipped, gray-black hair and a blunt manner that belied her soft heart. A prolific and beloved author, she was most famous for *Writing Down the Bones*, which she'd penned in a three-month frenzy in Santa Fe in 1986, after more than a decade practicing meditation and writing. Wisdom seemed to ooze out of her like a direct transmission from the sages, but she wasn't the usual blissed-out Buddha-type. She practically rattled with energy and laughter and often joked that I was her only friend who could match her zeal for life. Natalie became my unofficial mentor in writing and Zen, and in exchange, I taught her how to go up mountains in the dead of winter when neither of us felt like it. This, we joked, was my version of Zen.

Still, I should have known better than to ask Natalie for a definition. There's rarely a straight answer in Zen, and also every answer, in its own weird way, *is* a straight answer. Natalie tilted her head and was silent for a long moment, considering her response. "Wear black clothes to the Zendo," she said finally. "And loose. Baggy."

The night of the Dharma talk, I dressed carefully in wide-legged, dark-blue pants and a navy turtleneck sweater. I put on my warmest wool socks and winter boots. The snow had been falling all afternoon, piling up on the streets. Natalie phoned me, worried about driving. "We'll make it," I said confidently, secretly hoping no one else would.

The Zen center was nearly as dark as the road had been, lit by low lights along the perimeter, beautiful and peaceful. Winter boots were lined up neatly under a bench outside the door. Rosy-cheeked people in dark clothes sat on cushions on the floor, heads bowed in somber preparation for the meditation that would precede my talk. I sat on my cushion and tried to regulate my breathing and thought about the words I'd written and printed out like a speech, now crumpled into a useless ball in my pocket.

"I'll make it," I whispered to myself.

For the first time in my life, I found myself wishing that the meditation period would never end, that I would not have to get up and walk to the front of the room and try to remember what I'd come to say, what it was that I'd learned, and attempt to express it in words.

Two years earlier, I'd been in a terrible accident on a river in Idaho. I fell from a raft and was so badly injured I was told I should never run again.

I didn't listen.

I knew a little about brokenness. After my father died, I'd used my body to heal my mind, running long distances through the wilderness. Now I would have to use my mind to heal my body.

During my long recovery, Natalie gave me copy of the book *Zen Mind, Beginner's Mind*, by the late Japanese Zen master Shunryu Suzuki. I'd had surgery and was unable to walk for months. I felt as though I'd been dismantled, unmoored from my usual ways of moving through the world, like a stranger in my own skin.

"It's a classic, but you might not understand it," Natalie warned me. I didn't take it personally. Zen, by definition, is beyond definition, sometimes even description. As soon as I started reading, though, I understood everything. Not with my brain but in my body. I understood *Zen Mind* because I understood running.

I'd always been a runner. I ran through the woods when I was a girl, making up stories in my head. In my twenties, I ran through the sadness of breakups; in my thirties, I ran to write, and to find my feet beneath me in the deranged Tilt-a-whirl of new motherhood. I ran through the grief-fog of my father's death and the anxiety that nearly paralyzed me. I won ultramarathons (any race longer than 26.2 miles), and once I ran so hard I broke my own bone.

Running threaded through my whole life, but it was still only part of my life. In between the exhilarating highs were all the regular moments—gorgeous, ordinary moments, gorgeous often *because* they were so ordinary: wooden pins dangling on a clothes-line, the morning sun slanting across a chipped picket fence, my eight-year-old meticulously buttering her toast, ravens circling above a bald summit.

Suzuki Roshi described these bursts of understanding, these momentary awakenings, as "flashings in the vast phenomenal world." They're happening all around us, all the time—while we're eating an ice cream cone or riding our bike or sitting broken beside a river—but we're usually too distracted to notice. We don't have to be religious or spiritual or know how to meditate to experience these moments. We just have to pay attention and live wholeheartedly with what Suzuki Roshi called the "full quality of our being." When we do, we see the world and ourselves with sudden, brilliant clarity: we are part of everything, and everything is part of us.

Zen Mind, Beginner's Mind became my companion through my long recovery. It was disguised as a manual on meditation, but I felt as though I'd stumbled upon a set of secret instructions on how to live. "Each one of us must make his own true way, and when we do that, that way will express the universal way," Suzuki Roshi wrote.

It didn't matter if it was skydiving or capoeira, writing, running, or Zen. "When you understand one thing through and through, you understand everything."

The accident had upended everything and made me a beginner all over again. It was unclear if my body or my marriage would come through intact, or if I would ever run again. If I did, I would never run the same as I once had, just as I would never be the same.

Even then, part of me understood that this was a good thing, maybe the very best thing.

When the temple bell chimed, I got up and walked slowly to a metal chair in the front of the room. My talk was called "the Zen of Running," but to talk about running, I would have to talk about the river that broke me and the mountains that healed me.

I would have to talk about endings and beginnings, and how when you're in the middle, it's almost impossible to tell the two apart. Falling from the boat felt like a hard stop, a boulder rolled into the middle of a long tunnel, impassable. It was only after I healed that I saw my injury for what it was—a beginning wrapped around countless other beginnings. It was the start of something deeper, a spiritual practice, my own kind of wild Zen, an experiment in how to live and how to wake up to the brief flashings. They were so beautiful they took your breath away, and they were so easy to miss! I didn't want to miss them anymore.

Lifting my gaze, I looked at the faces before me. Their expressions were expectant but open, their bodies still but alert. They had come to receive something. All I had to do was offer it. Yet I couldn't tell them how to live, I could only tell them how I lived. I remembered something a person had once said to me. "You could share all your secrets and still not give everything away." I did not know him well, and would not know him for long, but I understood what he meant. We each have our own true way. We can imitate or be inspired, but we can only really ever be ourselves.

This is not a story about skydiving. Or capoeira. Of course you know that by now. It's not even really about running or Zen—nor marriage nor motherhood. And it's a book about all those things. I can't give you the six simple steps to enlightenment or the top ten tips to running faster. But I gladly offer you my secrets—and these brief flashings in the phenomenal world that crack open the sky and make us blink with wonder. The answers, if there are any, are yours to discover.

Part One

RIVERS

1. LESSONS IN FALLING

The first rule of rivers is the first rule of Zen. Don't fight the current. Go with it, not against it.

I know this. In the decades I've spent on rivers, I've learned this, sometimes the hard way. Often the hard way. And yet here I am, at the edge of a wild river in the remotest part of Idaho, at war with the water.

It's June 23, 2016, and my husband, Steve, and I are at the start of a six-day whitewater rafting trip down the Middle Fork of the Salmon, through a canyon so rugged it's called the River of No Return. The Middle Fork is one of the most premier wilderness trips in the country, famed for its clear, free-flowing river, trout-rich waters, natural hot springs, thrilling whitewater—one hundred major rapids in one hundred miles—and a remoteness that's unrivaled in the Lower Forty-Eight. The only way in or out is by boat, foot, horseback, or—in case of emergency—bush plane. Rafting access is strictly regulated to protect the wilderness. Getting a permit to float the Middle Fork without a guide, as our friends did, isn't like winning the lottery. It *is* winning the lottery.

The river is so loud we can hear it before we see it, a thunderous rush raging out of the high country. It's almost more frightening this way, like a cartoon waterfall lurking just around the next bend while you sail forth in a flimsy canoe, screaming "back paddle!" pointlesly over the din, only you can't because you've driven across four states in a day and crashed in a sleeping bag in your friend's backyard, and now you are here at the River of No Return, pretending to be brave.

I dip my toes in the frigid water and try to take a deep breath. Steve and I have given this trip to each other as an early tenth wedding anniversary present. We've been running rivers together even longer than we've been married, but this is by far the most technical whitewater we've ever rafted without a guide. I watch the rapids roiling over themselves, worry rising like a lump in my throat.

Then I remind myself that I'm with Steve, and that we do these things because we love them and because being afraid is rarely a good enough reason not to go. Fear belongs to a category of emotions we try not to talk about. If our marriage has an unofficial mission statement, this is it.

Rafts rigged, our group gathers on the beach to launch; then it's *one-two-three*, and we're pushing off, up to our ankles in the fifty-degree water, shoving ourselves out of the eddy. The current catches our inflatable raft with swift assurance, tugging us into the river's flow.

The Middle Fork of the Salmon is a pool-and-drop river, characterized by deep, calm water above each foaming rapid and another pool below it, the sequence repeating itself all the way downstream. Steve told me this at least a hundred times over the past few months, attempting to comfort me with the fact that if things go sideways in a hairball cataract, at least we'll have mellow water in which to collect ourselves and our gear. But this was not reassuring to me, not in the least. I knew what it *really* meant—that the rapids are huge and horrifying and can wreck you for real.

There's no time to think about any of this now, though, because there's not a single pool in sight, not this far up on the river's reach, so close to its headwaters in the Sawtooth Mountains. The current is unlike anything I've ever experienced, a choppy cascade of bony whitewater pouring swiftly through rocks. The water itself is a strange mix of green-black-clear, darkened by the forest shadows, spilling over itself like frothy soda foaming out of a shaken-up bottle. From where I sit in the bow, with Steve behind me on the oars, the rapids don't appear especially big, just constant—an unrelenting crash of whitewater disappearing around the first bend, narrow and fast.

I scan the river ahead for obstacles. There are too many to count, too many to call out, too much we don't know. We don't know that around the next bend is a pyramidal rock jabbing its pointed crown up from the middle of the river. We don't know that the rest of our group, now out of sight, has taken the left channel. We don't know that the current will suck us in to the rock like iron shavings onto a magnet or that Steve will think he has one more second than he does to take one more oar stroke to pull us off.

It all happens so fast. Maybe I say, "Do you see that rock?" with a sharpness to my voice that Steve might take to imply distrust. Maybe Steve answers, "Yes," in a hard, tight way that indicates we are coming upon it faster than he thought, or it upon us. Maybe I don't have time to say anything. I sense the tension in the way Steve is rowing, the way we seem to be resisting the river, pulling hard against it.

Then we're on it.

Instead of bouncing off the rock, as inflatable rafts often do, ours crumples against its face, blue rubber folding in on itself. We are not spinning free, we are not loosed back into the rapid. We are sideways against the rock. I'm on the high side, looking down at Steve, who yells, *"High Side!"* and clambers up beside me, hoping the shift in weight will release our boat from the swirl of current pinning us to the rock. For an instant, we hang there, perpendicular to the river at an angle so wrong I will do whatever I can to fight it. I climb higher on the rubber thwart. The angle is changing, but not in our favor. Now it's acute, tightening, the high side of the raft narrowing its gap with the water. Slowly, in what feels like quarter-time, we are falling over, falling in.

"Oh *fuuuuck!*" Steve yells, and there's no worse sound than these two words because Steve is always solid. He does not accidentally row into rocks. He does not freak out.

Steve's shout hangs in the air, the syllables elongated with terrible precision. Then, in a spin of elbow and knees, he's flopping into the water, churning white waves breaking on rocks, and I do the thing I know shouldn't: I hesitate. I hold on. I feel the strain in my neck, my arms, my thighs as I brace against the hard rubber floor of the raft. *I'm not falling, this is not happening.*

But it *is* happening.

Each fiber of my being is pinched tight, every muscle flexed, resisting gravity, resisting the river. I'm hanging in a moment that seems to stretch on forever. *Let go*, my brain screams, as my body does the opposite. It's futile, but I'm fighting it. I know I shouldn't, but I am.

I've taught myself to run up mountains, but I don't know how to fall.

2. CONSTANCY

All month before we left for Idaho, I ran up the same mountain every day. Running up a mountain and running a river aren't so different, actually. You're part of an energy that's bigger and wilder than your own. You have to run the same way water flows. You have to move with the mountain, not against it.

The sun was barely pulling itself up over the crest of the mountain when I slipped out of the house on the first of June, still half asleep, a banana in one hand, car keys in the other. At just after six, the morning was already warm and bright, a late spring day like any other in Santa Fe. Beginnings almost always seem ordinary at the time. Only later, from a distance, can you see how what appeared to be an unremarkable decision marked the start of something that would shift the course of what was to come. What, unaware, you had begun.

Dawn is the best time to start. The whole day lies before you, before the promise of the morning dies at the hand of to-do lists, phone calls, before your husband asks, "What's the balance in our joint checking account?" and your heart sags a little because you really can't say, and the sun begins its long, inevitable slant toward the other horizon.

I never planned to run up our local mountain, Atalaya, every day, I only wanted to run up it that day. I was looking for answers. They rose up like pebbles between my toes; they flowed down like the sap that ran thick and sweet through the ponderosa trees; many days, they came as words strung together in the right order, like beads on a string, plucked from the sky. The answers came from all around, from the sound of my heart beating in my chest and from the ravens calling overhead. When I ran this way, running felt like writing, and writing like running.

I liked being out in the early caramel light. I liked how I could feel my body working with the hill, how my pace and effort adjusted naturally to the incline, and I liked coming home salt-filmed and sweaty, carrying the trail with me, and pouring it into my writing: the wrinkled bark and the blue sky wavy with clouds, the lone plane streaking overhead leaving a trail, the gray, tufted-ear squirrel darting between trees, the pine needles like a carpet, softening my footsteps.

Running at dawn was so satisfying, I did it the next morning, and the next. After three days, I had a little streak going. That's what runners call it when they run every day for many days, or years, in a row. The longest-running active streak belongs to seventy-three-year-old Jon Sutherland from Utah, who's been running every day for 20,114 days and counting—more than fifty-five years.

A streak has a natural length, a clear beginning and end. The important thing is to let it be what it will be without forcing it. This is the tricky part. Though the definition of a streak is unbroken effort, every streak is meant to end. If you get too stubborn to let it go, you'll kill the thing it's supposed to teach you. You don't necessarily know what this is while you're in the middle of the streak, but once it's over and you have some distance from it, the lesson may become clear. If you think you understand the meaning of the streak while you're doing it, think again.

I'd never run a streak before or even thought of doing one, but after five days, I couldn't imagine *not* running up the mountain. It wasn't the novelty of it. It was the fact that I didn't have to decide. Doing the same thing every day is easier than having to choose what to do, until it becomes harder, and that's when you know it's time to do something different. It made me think of the Zen saying, "The way isn't hard to follow. Just avoid picking and choosing."

Because I didn't have to expend energy choosing where to run, my way was clear. Up the mountain and back down again. I could usually make it back in time to help make our daughters, Pippa and Maisy, breakfast and get ready for summer camp. They were five and seven that summer, and sometimes they'd just be waking up when I got home.

By the end of the first week, my quads were sore, and my Achilles tendons had begun to balk at the daily 1,800-foot climb up the mountain. Still, I had no plans to stop, even though I knew at some point I must. I just didn't know yet how it would end. I didn't stop after ten days when my ankles were so tight they felt like coiled springs. Not after I tripped over a root and skinned my knee on a rock. I washed the dirt from the abrasion, got up the next morning, and went back to the mountain; I memorized the root and kept an eye out for it so I didn't fall again.

I was writing a book about my father that summer, and running up the mountain was how I got to my desk each day. Like most rituals, it contained an element of superstition; if I ran up Atalaya and had a good day writing, then I had to do it again the next day to ensure the same result. Superstitions are entertaining, but at their core they imply a lack of trust: you think you depend on consistent, external elements in order to produce your best work, when in fact, it comes from within.

A central principle of Zen is constancy—making continuous effort. This is the Buddhist version of a streak. You show up every day to meet your life as it is, no matter the weather, your mood, whether you want to or not. You build a structure around meditation—where you sit, when, and for how long—and you keep going. You can make anything a continuous practice, an expression of constancy—running up a mountain or writing a book or baking bread.

"We cannot keep still," Suzuki Roshi wrote. "We have to do something. So if you do something, you should be very observant and careful, and alert. Put the dough in the oven and watch it carefully. Once you know how the dough becomes bread, you will understand enlightenment."

Running up the mountain was putting the dough in the oven every day and watching it rise. Gradually it would become something different, I just didn't know what.

—

I'd spent all winter and early spring training for a race, a hundred-kilometer ultramarathon in the hills outside of San Francisco. Though I'd run the distance once, a year earlier, it seemed foolish, implausible. There are two ways to interpret such trepidation: one is to be frightened, the other curious. I decided that my inability to imagine myself running sixty-two miles was a good sign: it meant that running was fresh for me again, that nothing was assumed, and therefore anything was possible.

I decided to believe this.

Many days I ran across a dry, dusty mesa just outside of Santa Fe, eight miles east of the Rio Grande. The mesa is mostly level, with small rolling hills and negligible elevation change. The trees there are bushes, really, hardly higher than my head, and offer very little shade. Some days it was unpleasant and windy, and I would set out to get it over with as fast as I could. I'd flick my wrist a dozen times a minute to see if I was running a 7:54 pace or 8:01. If I could rush through my run, I'd be done for the day. I could go home and write and get to school by three o'clock to meet the girls, who were growing so fast they'd soon no longer need me to walk them home. I had to hurry to be with them, and then I had to slow time so it wouldn't end.

This was impossible, of course. It would never work. Trying would only bring me more heartache.

Success in running is measured by speed, but I'd always struggled with this aspect of it. Ever since I was young, running had been a way of writing and seeing—a way to slow time and slide inside of it. It was like a magic trick: your body could be running fast, but your mind was moving very slowly, opening wide and inhaling the world. If I wasn't careful, racing would strangle the very thing I loved most about running.

So instead of focusing on miles or minutes or mountains while I ran, I began to think about rivers. The one I imagined in my mind was bright and clear, olive green, corkscrewing through a deep canyon, reflecting the sky. I knew this river. It was all the rivers I had ever floated, and all the rivers I wanted to still. The river cut through the canyon, and the canyon was cut through by the river; the process was natural and powerful and very slow and moved in both directions. You couldn't see it happening. You had to trust that it was.

The river was never in any hurry, one way or the other. If I could slot into time the way the river fit into its canyon, I wouldn't have to worry about pace, about pushing too hard or going too slowly. I would be exactly in time. The river *was* time.

When I ran like the river, I felt as though I'd located a secret gear—not necessarily faster, but smoother. I settled into a slot in time. The air flowed around me, or I flowed through the air. The dust whirled about my face, but I didn't feel it. Running in this way was as close to liquid as I could get—carried along with no resistance at the right and peaceful speed, like a stick in the current that drifts by without a ripple.

—

I wrote late at night, after the girls had gone to sleep, when the house was still and quiet, even just a few sentences, so I stayed with the story. Many nights I dreamed about sentences. Sometimes I woke at 3:00 a.m. with a word in my head and rolled over quietly, switched on my headlamp, and wrote it down as fast as I could so I didn't disturb Steve. Sleeping was one of the things we did best together. We didn't have to talk, we just lay with our arms and legs wrapped around each other all night, snugged tightly into place like gears in a motor.

When I woke in the morning to go for a run, I could feel my mind working on the story, and the mountain working on it, too. I ran as though hypnotized, in a fog of unspecified thinking that was due in part to the earliness of the hour and the exertion required to run up the mountain. Motion quieted my superficial, analytical monologue; I could hear what my subconscious had to say.

By the second week of running up Atalaya, the soreness in my calves had dissipated, and I was no longer creaky when I got out of the car at the trailhead. My legs were quick and my feet skipped over the rocks and dirt, floating uphill. I was beating the same well-worn path to the top of the mountain, but it was different every day. The unremitting sameness revealed in fact that nothing was the same, ever. The light was golden and cloudless; other days a soft wind rose behind the peak, swirled over the summit, and rolled down the front, cold air draining with it. I was in that phase where I thought it could go on forever. Everything was known, but nothing was tedious, the running and the mountain and the writing, all of it fitting together. There was only one problem. Steve and I were leaving for Idaho in a week.

—

The hundred-kilometer race started before dawn, the sky speckled with stars. We climbed up a long ravine, single file on a narrow trail that gained a mountainous slope, hundreds of headlights strung out. On the summit, a bagpipe player greeted us and the rising sun with a song. It was light enough to see the ocean, choppy and beautiful and blue. I fell into pace with a woman, near the front. We talked a bit and were silent for long stretches. The trail wended its way up and down bucolic open hillsides, past a Zen center with enormous eucalyptus trees and long views of the sea. My body was on the mountain, but my mind was running like the river.

By late morning, though, the sea began to vanish into clouds. The clouds were thicker than fog, more definitive. It was a storm. At the next aid station, the woman I'd been running with was greeted by her sponsor's van and dashed back onto the trail as I pawed hurriedly through my gear bag. Frazzled and alone again, I left in a rush without my jacket and gloves. Not twenty minutes later, it began to sleet. I became very cold. Soon my bare arms and legs were pink and numb, barely able to bend. I grew worried, reviewed my options:

I would ask a volunteer at the next aid station for gloves.

Maybe there would be hot soup.

I would ask another runner for spare clothes.

There was one up ahead. He wore white compression socks pulled up to his knees. They were now splattered and filthy with mud.

I kept him and his socks in sight. We were on a high ridge, traversing it slowly from south to north. It should have been stunning, but I couldn't see more than ten feet in front of me. Though it was May, it was forty degrees with a biting wind. Cold stabbed like knives into my thighs. I'd thought the day would get warmer as it got later, but I'd been wrong.

White socks and I leapfrogged along the trail. I passed him on the climbs, he caught me on the descents. He was the only person in sight, and I felt for him a growing tenderness. I continued to bargain with myself. If things got really bad, I would ask Lance—we had introduced ourselves by then—if he had an extra layer.

I thought this was a good sign. I was making contingency plans even as my body turned into a hard slab of sea ice, even as the trail turned to water, rain drummed sideways, and I was so cold I could no longer think straight.

Where was the river now? Where had it gone?

Oh.

The river was in the sky.

Afterward, when it was finally over and I'd run off the ridge and down a thousand vertical feet to the fifty-mile aid station, where it had stopped raining, was marginally warmer, and I'd seen my sister, Meg, and been met by my friend Anna, who would pace me to the finish (I lurched on worthless legs to finish third), I learned that half the field had dropped out behind me, many with hypothermia.

Not long after, Lance staggered across the finish line in his brown socks. I went over to congratulate him and told him that for miles I'd been trying to get up my nerve to ask him for a jacket but wasn't brave enough.

"I would have given you mine," he said, smiling.

I told Lance what I'd learned: the rain was actually lucky for us. It was only because we'd been running just ahead of the storm—in front of the hail and icy wind—that we'd been able to push through it. I *had* run like the river. I'd been liquid after all.

Sometimes the river flows through canyons and sometimes it falls from the sky.

Mid-June. It rains before dawn and the trail up the mountain is tacky and sweet, the dust still wet. Raindrops glitter like tears on the tips of the piñon needles, happy tears. In New Mexico, rain is a gift. One set of footprints stamps the soggy earth ahead of me.

On the summit, the blur of a body materializes out of the mist. It's my friend Carol. We hug, and I tell her I am running up the mountain every day. "I'm not entirely sure why," I add, "but I am."

Carol doesn't hesitate. "Because it's your mountain," she says.

It's not my mountain, of course. It's all of ours and none of ours; it's the ancestral homeland of those who'd come before. It is itself. The most famous Zen master of all, Eihei Dogen, a Japanese poet-philosopher who lived in the thirteenth century, once wrote, "Mountains belong to people who love them." I've known Atalaya so well and loved it for so long, it feels like mine. But the opposite is true: I belong to the mountain.

3. FLOW

I always fell in love on rivers.

The first time, I was twenty-four and had lived in Santa Fe for a year. A boy I knew tied two whitewater kayaks to the roof of his car and drove us to the Rio Chama, a swift-moving tributary that carves through the red rock canyon where Georgia O'Keeffe once lived and painted. I'd learned to paddle my mother's wooden canoe when I was six, grew up sailing small dinghies on a lake, and sea kayaked with my father down the calm water of the Connecticut River, but I had never before wedged my body into a small plastic hull on rapids big enough to flip a boat. It seemed wildly imprudent.

On the shore, the boy handed me a wetsuit and discreetly averted his eyes while I stripped down to my bathing suit and squeezed the stiff neoprene up over my thighs. The river rushed by, pillowing over rocks that jabbed through the surface like sharks. I looked at the kayaks, as flimsy as bath toys. The riverbanks were thick with sagebrush, and I inhaled their sweet perfume to calm myself—a scent I would, from then on, associate with the rush of love, adventure, and a spark of fear. The longer I lived in New Mexico, the more entwined these feelings would become.

Rivers always look different from above. You can see their long twisting bends, the arc of their path through the canyon, the way the water follows the path of least resistance, which is constantly changing, even if it's so incremental you can't detect it. On the river you see only the bend you're on, not the headwaters nor the delta. There are always so many more bends than you expect. The shortest distance between two points is a straight line, not a river.

Rivers are a lesson in constancy and impermanence, a true contradiction: snow becomes runoff becomes rivers, empties to the sea or is diverted to farm fields, is absorbed by plants, is offered to the world as oxygen, returns to the earth as water or snow, hail, or ice, and flows again into rivers. Rivers appear to move in one direction, downstream, but their path is circular, infinite.

I like this about rivers.

Somehow I managed to stay upright in my boat that first day, though I was far from graceful. I stabbed frenetically at the river with my paddle until an afternoon thunderstorm chased us off the water, and the boy and I dragged our boats through the sagebrush and out to the dirt road, where we walked back to his car. From the safety of shore, I watched the current swirl steadily past us, mesmerized. There seemed to be no end to the water. Where did it come from and where was it going?

Another summer: riding my bicycle at dusk along a ribbon of asphalt beside a river so clear you could see all the way to the pebbly bottom. The Douglas firs were huge and smelled damp, like snow in the high country that had only recently melted. Fat pink salmon swam in the deepest pools, ink blue and cold. I pumped my pedals hard to get back in time for dinner. I was more confident in my kayak now. I was learning to capsize on purpose and roll my boat upright while I was upside-down in the water. Over and over, I practiced snapping my hips while sweeping my paddle in a C-shape around the overturned hull. Every afternoon I ate an ice cream sandwich, licking the sides as it dripped into my palm. I was hungry all the time, in love with the river, and with something I had only just discovered: my own wildness.

This was the summer of 2000, the summer I met Steve. The era of nineties excess was over, Y2K hysteria had fizzled out, the world seemed more or less stable, and everything still felt like the beginning, wide open and full of opportunities, like the 00's stretching forward in the numbers of the new millennium.

Into this summer walked Steve. The moment I saw him, I knew I would love him. Maybe I already did.

In my mind, I am always this age on rivers: twenty-eight, a girl with a freckled nose and shoulders strong and lean from paddling.

A girl who knows it is possible to be afraid and euphoric in the same breath, who's learning that the most important thing on any river is ease. You need momentum, not brute strength, to move downstream. You have to be fluid, not forceful. If you fight it, you'll never win. You have to flow.

—

A year after Steve and I began dating, we bought a canoe. It had woven cane seats and a sturdy hull designed for whitewater. On our maiden voyage, down the Rio Grande, Steve climbed into the stern and I sat in the bow. I was responsible for paddling, Steve for steering, maneuvering us through boulders flung by gravity into the riverbed. I was power, he was precision.

From the outset, I balked at the bow. It struck me as demeaning. Once, early on, Steve and I got into a shouting match as we bounced downstream, banging into rocks. Afterward, I called my mother. "He thinks he's the boss," I groaned. She assured me that this didn't mean Steve was sexist, only that he wanted to get us downriver safely. She'd been raised to believe that women could do anything men could do, and usually better. She believed this so adamantly she couldn't fathom my irritation. We women were so capable, we should be above being bothered by riding in the bow.

Never mind that she always sat the in stern in her own canoe.

Looking back, this was our first real power struggle, the one that would play out on different rivers as the years unfolded. Our fights were always about the same thing: control. Rivers brought it out in us. Steve and I had both been raised on the East Coast, on lakes, and were still learning how to navigate rivers. I suppose we each wanted to claim dominance while pretending that we weren't just a little out of our league.

The first overnight river trip we took together was down the Green River, in 2002. The Green flows more than 700 miles from its headwaters in Wyoming's Wind River range, south through Utah to its confluence with the Colorado River. Its name refers not to the color of the water, which, like most desert tributaries, is a thick, sludge-like brown, but to the vegetation that grows along its banks. Near the end of its reach is Labyrinth Canyon, forty-five miles of flat water snaking through 500-foot sandstone walls. Steve and I planned to take four days to run Labyrinth in our canoe—an exercise in total commitment, a not-so-dry run.

At the boat launch an hour north of Moab, the canoe was so laden with food and bodies and camping gear that the gunwales were an inch above water; our dog, Gus, tucked himself into the cramped space between Steve's knees. The shuttle driver, Dan, who we'd paid to drive us to the river and pick us up in four days at Mineral Bottom, narrowed his eyes and laughed twitchily. "It's hard to tell if you're sinking or floating!" Then, before we could change our minds, he pointed downstream and bellowed, "Head thataway! You're on river time now!"

The current through the canyon was steady, moving with impressive purpose at three or four miles an hour, roughly the pace of walking. But our canoe was so heavy and had so much momentum, we soon guessed we were going closer to five miles an hour. It was ninety degrees in early September, and the river was warm and still as a bath but reddish brown, the color of the desert dirt that washes down the side canyons when it storms. Every so often we took turns pitching over the side of the canoe into the water to cool off. The river was so gentle we could have floated the whole canyon on our backs if we'd wanted to.

By late afternoon, bruise-bottomed storm clouds began to mass in the narrowing wedge of sky. The river had so many bends, it was hard to tell if we were moving toward the clouds or away from them. Then the wind picked up, stirring the calm water into whitecaps that blew us back upstream, and we had our answer.

"Paddle to shore!" Steve yelled needlessly above the roar—the wind was slamming us there, like it or not.

The weather changes quickly in the high desert, especially in summer, when high temperatures create afternoon thunderstorms. We were used to this from Santa Fe, where sudden teeming squalls drop temperatures twenty degrees in five minutes, send hail lashing sideways, and flood arroyos with the moisture the arid soil cannot absorb.

We hopped out in an ankle-deep eddy and heaved the canoe onto a narrow slip of willowy beach only a foot or two above the water line. The sky had gone graphite and terrible, and Steve shouted for us to empty the boat and pull it onto higher ground, into the willows. Just as we set it down, a gale roared upstream as though shot straight out of belly of the storm, pelting our bare skin with a fury of sand and grit.

All at once, the wind picked up our canoe and tossed it into the air.

For a moment, it hovered in the sky above our heads while we stared, mouths agape, arms rising in self-defense. Just as suddenly, the wind shifted and released its grip, and the canoe hit the ground a few feet away with a sickening thud.

For half an hour, we huddled with Gus under the overturned boat while the storm battered the canyon. Even as we clutched at the cane seats to keep the boat from flying into the sky as it strained against our grip, we stayed very still and quiet, listening and feeling for shifts that might signal the storm's end. It was too loud to talk, but I could tell we were thinking the same thing: If we lost our canoe, how would we make it out?

When at last the sky brightened, we crawled out to assess the damage. Our gear was scattered in the willows, the canoe badly scratched but intact. We had grit in every orifice: ears, nose, the corners of our eyes, between our toes, bellybuttons, fingernails. Gus was a raccoon masquerading as a dog, his eyes ringed with sand, pixilated yellow moons through which he blinked incredulously. The air was still, the sky resuming its normal shade of cyan blue. But we'd been changed. We'd come through something together, in a wild place with no contingencies, and the close call sealed us.

Afterward, the sky scrubbed clear of clouds, we took our time drifting downstream. It was so hot we stripped off all our clothes and threw the Frisbee on pearly sandbars and ran up side canyons in our river sandals and spread our sleeping bags on the sand to read dog-eared paperbacks and watch the stars pop out.

On our last morning, I lay on the sand in my bathing suit, the sun warming my bare skin. The willows smelled sweet. We had three long bends in the river, maybe four, before we'd reach Mineral Bottom, where, with any luck, our ride would be waiting. I thought of the other times I'd fallen in love on rivers, and how the end of the river had also, in a way, meant the end of us. But this time, with Steve, was different. I could feel it in the way we were together, steady and easy—almost ordinary, the very best kind of ordinary—and in how the days stretched out before us, calm and hot and without constraint. We had all the time we needed. We wouldn't have to give up anything. We wouldn't have to choose. We would leave the river, but not each other.

We could stay together, like this, forever.

4. BOREDOM

Running up the same mountain every day was getting boring, as I knew it would. I'd crossed an invisible threshold; the novelty had worn off, and the ritual was on the brink of becoming stale. Some mornings I wanted to stay in bed with Steve or read a book before getting up, rather than dash out at first light. The trail up Atalaya had become so familiar I barely noticed it anymore. The mornings were the longest they'd be all year, and the light was peachy and tinged with haze from a forest fire 300 miles away in Arizona. The blaze was so far away we couldn't smell the smoke, but it bathed the landscape in a rosy glow, softening the edges. Fire sky.

I thought of someone who'd told me about a Zen koan that goes, "How do you put out a fire that is ten miles away?" He'd finally solved it, he said. I could tell he wanted to explain it to me, even though by their very nature, Zen koans are enigmatic, illuminating ancient stories of awakening that defy intellectual interpretation or reason. You're not supposed to give away the answers. You're supposed to penetrate the koans yourself, not by thinking but by not thinking.

But he seemed so eager, I couldn't resist. I took the bait. "How?" I asked him.

"You become the fire."

When you do anything repetitively, for a long time, the ritual inevitably begins to lose some of its impact. If it's physical, your body adapts to the challenge, and the noticeable gains you experienced begin to plateau. You're still progressing, but more slowly. Mentally, you may start to question the activity's meaning, which only days or weeks before had seemed so clear.

It's natural to think about quitting. It would have been easy to justify. Running up the mountain every day didn't make sense. I was supposed to be training for another hundred-kilometer race in Vermont, at an elevation of a couple thousand feet. As a competitive ultra runner, I should have varied my training runs to avoid burning out, tailored my routes for the next race. I should have sought out faster and flatter terrain to improve my speed, taken a rest day each week. That's what any serious, smart runner would have done.

But it was summer, and all the snow had finally melted, and I could go out in shorts and a sports bra. I didn't want to be smart or good. I wanted to run in the mountains until I ran out of daylight. I wanted to meet boredom with boredom and find out what's on the other side.

Become the fire.

—

Childhood in the 1980s was one long yawning chasm of boredom. You had to think of things to do or you would go out of your mind with the tedium of unstructured freedom. There were no screens, no internet, no on-demand TV—just *Three's Company* at six every night, long rows of *Encyclopedia Britannica* on the shelves in the den, and all the library books we could lug home on our bikes.

On days when we were flattened by the monotony of suburbia, awash in the torpor of early adolescence, my stepsister, Amy, and I would make up games. She was nine months older than me and liked every kind of game that existed. If it didn't exist, we invented it. We were pioneer girls with our fake horse. We pushed through my mother's long woolen coats in the upstairs closet with a theatrical flair, sure we'd find a hidden doorway to Narnia. We were paraplegics injured in a horrible accident who'd lost the use of our legs and had to save ourselves from a sinking ship. We crawled up and down the front stairs using only our elbows, our legs pretzeled in full lotus. Orphanhood permeated nearly every plot line. In place of our parents, there were sisters, friends, cousins. The more complex the web of interconnection, the better. This was the unspoken objective of our games: we liked to figure out how everyone fit together, probably because we were still trying to figure out how we did.

My imagination was my most reliable source of entertainment. It was independent of other people and circumstances, highly portable, and, best of all, private. After Amy went home to her mom's house on Sunday afternoons, I would ride my bike down the street by myself, and no one would know I was making up stories in my head, worlds that only I inhabited. But I could show them. I could tell them. Boredom was the beginning of writing.

Now, after ten months of working on my book, I'd hit that dreaded lull—the initial thrill had worn off, and I was still so far from the end I couldn't even think about the end. It wasn't my book that bored me as much as the voices in my head when I sat down to write. *Who will care? This story has been written so many times before, and better than you. What's so special about losing a father?* These are the most unimaginative voices imaginable. Everyone has them.

I had to find a way to make writing fresh again, to feel a spark for the thing I'd loved my whole life, longer even than I'd loved running. The glamour was gone. I just had to put my head down and make it work.

Zen meditation, or *zazen*, has been described as a "lonesome monotony." Sometimes running feels this way, too: the same repetitive motion, day after day after day, alone with your thoughts. Even when I'm not on a streak, I'm a creature of habit, sometimes even a slave to my habits. The sheer repetition is enough to make me fantasize about taking up a new sport—open water swimming!—or buying a bike. I long to be normal. But I don't, not really. I just long to be myself.

Fatigue was inescapable. The consoling outlines of routine had devolved into dullness. Could I find the place where boredom blossomed into ritual, mindlessness into attention? Could I draw inspiration from repetition? I knew I wouldn't find the answer in my head, but on the mountain and in the forest and in the way I moved my body on the mountain.

I kept running.

—

A few months earlier, my uncle had died. Philip was my father's only sibling, four years younger, and intellectually disabled since birth. He was seventy-three, the same age my father had been when he died.

At Phil's memorial service in upstate New York, a Quaker minister spoke about "infinite love" as the force that created the big bang. When you think of the scope of the universe, he explained, and all the billions of stars in the cosmos—just flickering pinpricks of light, cosmos within cosmos—the distance between Phil and someone of exceptional brilliance and physical strength was almost nil. There was, as the Zen saying goes, a hair's breadth of difference between the two.

What it comes down to, he continued, is the remarkable, insistent will of living beings to survive. Blades of grass and trees and humans like Phil. He'd faced so many obstacles in life, more than most of us, and yet he'd persevered, quietly and without fanfare.

The minister paused and looked down at Phil's simple gravestone, engraved with his name and, in one corner, a small bicycle. My father had bought him one, and Phil liked to ride all around. "So you see," the minister concluded, "it's in our nature to just keep going."

After that, I thought about Phil when I ran up the mountain. I thought about his pipe and his checkered driving cap and his bicycle and how my father had often become impatient with him, and what that must have felt like, and the Christmas cards he'd sent from Wisconsin, written in his shaky penmanship, and how I hadn't known him in a long time, since I was a child. Did he have small, happy moments? Was he bored? What brought him pleasure? Had he passed some of his resilience on to the rest of us?

And I thought about my own boredom—in writing and running, motherhood and marriage—which, I was realizing, wasn't really boredom but a lack of imagination, or appreciation. Maybe even stamina. What I needed was to stay with it all, with the tedium and uncertainty and discomfort, just as Phil had. Maybe this was its own kind of freedom.

—

After I ran down Atayala every morning, I'd sit in the backyard and try to meditate. I had started to learn how a decade earlier, in the months following my father's death, when I was convinced I was dying, too. In my quest for calm, I tried all sorts of methods: *vipassana* (insight meditation), mindfulness meditation, *metta* (loving-kindness meditation), Zen. Of all the forms, I liked Zen the best. Zazen was the simplest; it means "just sitting." I didn't have to remember a mantra or follow prompts. I didn't have to study texts. I just had to settle my body and breathe.

When Natalie and I hiked together up the mountain, she often sat alone on a ledge halfway up while I climbed another mile to the summit. On my way back down, I'd find her with her eyes closed and her back straight as a ruler against a ponderosa, her body an exact imitation of the mountain, a look of utter blankness on her face. Her expression was beyond calmness or tranquility. It was emptiness itself.

Natalie learned zazen from her teacher, a Japanese Zen master named Dainin Katagiri, in St. Paul, Minnesota, in the 1980s. He came from a long lineage of Soto Zen priests in the tradition of Eihei Dogen. Like Dogen, Katagiri Roshi taught that zazen is a way of facing into the reality of life and cultivating a peaceful mind. It is how we express what he called "universal energy"—our interconnection with all beings.

Every meditation teacher I encountered had a different style, and my way became an amalgamation of theirs. I taught myself to sit anywhere: beside a river, on top of the mountain, in our backyard beside a fountain that sounded the teeniest bit like a river way off in the distance. I bought a small round cushion, or *zafu*, to sit on, but sometimes I forgot to bring it in when it rained, and it started molding around the seams. *So not Zen*, I thought shamefully. Katagiri Roshi used to tell his students, "Take care of your life," meaning don't be sloppy, attend to the details, large and small. If you had to reduce Zen to a few simple teachings, this would be a big one.

One morning, through downcast eyes, I noticed a blade of grass swaying in the breeze. It looked as though it was waving at me. I narrowed my gaze.

Inhaled, exhaled.

There it was again. The grass was cerulean, newborn green, recently sprung from the warming earth, trying to get my attention.

I looked closely. The single blade of bright green grass contained an entirely separate life. A life where I lived in a bungalow in a town with wide city streets and big trees. Cowboys at the pizza parlor on the street along the railroad tracks.

All of this flickered before me when I was not supposed to be thinking. These weren't thoughts, though, but sensations, or maybe memories of something that hadn't yet happened but lived inside my unconscious. They felt like waking up from a dream with a warm, sweet feeling that lasts all day.

After a few moments, I went inside to write down what I'd seen. I could picture these other lives so clearly they almost scared me. It would be easy to want something different, new. Steve and I had been married for ten years, together for sixteen. We had all the same arguments. We told all the same inside jokes about our life, the time X and Y, the jokes only we thought were funny. Sometimes I wanted to tackle him in a long hug and rub his short hair that he cut himself, in the bathroom with a straight razor, never quite managing to get the line straight. But did I? Not as often as I used to.

Life was full, one thing after the next. Daughters and writing and running and dishes, there were so many dirty dishes. Always when I pictured our life together, I saw mountains and tents beside rivers and trails twisting above tree line, but I also saw dishes. The same pile in the same place. Steve is the cook in our family, so dishes were my job, but did I do them? Not always. Increasingly, no.

We live our lives in our imaginations but also in the kitchen, amidst the dirty dishes and calendars with too many things to do, and in the backyard, coaxing order out of chaos, our feet on the ground right in the middle of the mess, even as we long to be free.

I hadn't gone looking for the blade of grass, it had found me. And where would it lead? Into exponentially more fantastic and intricate worlds and back around to here, nowhere but here, exactly this moment, where I am and have always been.

I bent over my notebook, scattered cherry pits and a half-drunk cup of tea beside me on the kitchen table, the dog chewing a bone at my feet. Steve, on his cell phone giving instructions in Spanish to his work crew, grinned good morning at me with his dimples. This was life, my life.

The lonesome monotony of it all. Also, the joy.

—

The next morning I woke to birds calling me out of bed and into the orange sky. I worked my way up the mountain. I knew all the sections, one by one they came and went, the dirt road to start, the rolling respite after the first climb, the steep crux near the top. Along the summit ridge, where you can stop focusing on your feet and gaze into the folds of the mountains stretching east and north, across the Santa Fe watershed, and beyond to the high peaks.

Lavender penstemon bloomed alongside the trail. A raven hopped onto a rock. The bird was enormous, regal, the size of a small cat. It held something tan in its mouth. I edged closer to investigate. I could see the bird's glossy feathers fanned out like a deck of cards, a pinon nut between its beak. Unperturbed, the bird eyed me boldly, then it lifted its wings and flew.

On the way down, my arms swinging loosely at my sides, I suddenly saw it clearly—the unknowable, far-away future, still a mystery save for this fact: I may not always be fast, but it doesn't matter as long as I have this—running free down a mountain, ideas spilling out of my head, so many I can't hold them all. My speed might not last, but with any luck, the stories will.

In the past month on Atalaya I'd seen everything, and stopped noticing, and now I was paying attention again. I had boredom to thank. It taught me how to see this morning, maybe the most beautiful one of all, because it was my last. It's strange how we miss things the most just as they're about to end.

5. THE SUMMER I DIDN'T DIE

We were leaving for Idaho. Steve packed the raft and coolers. I packed our gear and a stack of books—there are few simpler pleasures than lying in a tent beside a river, turning pages by headlamp.

The best book I'd ever read on a river wasn't about rivers, it was about ranches. In Labyrinth Canyon on the Green River with Steve, Gretel Ehrlich's *The Solace of Open Spaces* lopped the top right off of my head. Ehrlich was grieving love when on a whim she moved to Wyoming's ranch country. Her story reminded me a little of my own relocation to New Mexico when I was twenty-three. I was only supposed to stay for three months, six tops. But nine years later, I was still here.

I had lain on sandbars in the late afternoon, entranced by Ehrlich's book. Not because I knew about horses or because I felt an affinity for the sagebrush plains of Wyoming or its crack-skinned cowboys, but because she represented something to me: the courage to leave the life you thought you were meant to have for one you never expected and sometimes weren't sure you wanted, but were drawn to nonetheless. Ehrlich embodied an enviable blend of conviction and openness to deep uncertainty, the kind most of us resist because it's too uncomfortable. She threw herself into it in Wyoming. For much of the book she didn't know what she was doing, where she was going, or even who she was—until she did. She wrote her way into knowing.

For our trip down the Middle Fork, I wanted something wild and literary, writing as daring and rugged as the Idaho wilderness. I spent a long time in the bookstore before I finally settled on a novella by the Montana writer Jim Harrison called *The Summer He Didn't Die*. The title gave me a little shiver of foreboding. I wasn't sure about my choice. I remember this. I wasn't sure, but I bought it anyway.

In my mind, the ambivalence I felt about the book has become conflated with, or equated to, the ambivalence I felt about the trip. I was excited to get away with Steve, to spend a week together in a wild and stunning wilderness. Steve planned to fly-fish whenever he wasn't rowing, and I couldn't wait to run the singletrack that parallels the river. In the nearly eight years Steve and I had been parents, we'd gotten away two, maybe three times without the girls. We could float untethered from our parental duties, free.

But.

There was the water, bigger water than we'd ever paddled together. One hundred major rapids in one hundred miles, many of them rated Class IV on the whitewater scale (Class V is the highest); people drown in the Middle Fork every year.

It was both good and bad that we weren't bringing the girls. You always want it both ways, as a mother. *Please leave me alone. Please never leave me.* That, I suppose, is the definition of parenthood. Knowing Pippa and Maisy were too small to come along, or rather that the river was too big, scared me; it meant the Middle Fork was serious business, which we knew, I knew—had been thinking about for months, ever since our friends emailed us in February to say they'd gotten a permit.

The Middle Fork had been at the top of our wish list since we bought our raft in 2008, the summer Pippa was born. Thirteen feet long, the raft was big enough to haul the three of us, a dog, and the small mountain of gear required to travel in the backcountry with a baby. When Pippa was eight weeks old, we took her down her first river, a short, calm day stretch on the Rio Chama. Steve rowed while I sat under a flimsy beach umbrella, holding Pippa in my arms. We pulled ashore above the rapids so I could get out and carry her safely around the whitewater. When it comes to risk,

Steve and I are both naturally conservative, but my tolerance for danger dropped noticeably once I became a mother.

Even after Maisy was born, we tried to get out on several river trips each summer. We were training ourselves, as much as our daughters, to endure discomfort and unknowns, inclement weather, and physical and mental challenges. We wanted Pippa and Maisy to feel at home in nature, to cultivate a lifelong relationship with the world's wildness and their own. We didn't need Class IV whitewater to do this. We just needed time together, outside.

Then, out of nowhere, the invitation arrived. Could we get away for a week in June to go to the Middle Fork? Steve and I looked at each other, eyes wide with our good fortune, our brains already buzzing with logistics. There were so many details we'd have to sort out, but we'd already decided. Every year thousands of people apply to float the river; only a fraction are chosen at random. Who knew when we'd get another chance?

—

June 22, 2016. Steve and I wake before sunup for the sixteen-hour drive to Sun Valley. In the photo of us beside the truck, Steve's arm is around me and we are smiling expectantly, waiting for my mother, who's come to babysit, to take the picture. She is impatient, urging us away, swatting her hands as if she wants us to get the leaving over with. It would be so easy to stay home and be with my mother and run up the mountain and let Steve have his own freedom, the way I've had mine all month on Atalaya. But the girls are standing on the back steps in their pajamas and bare feet, jumpy with excitement, waving goodbye, and it's too late to change my mind, so I blow them kisses and climb into the cab.

As we ease down the driveway, I turn to Steve and, lowering my voice an octave for dramatic effect, say, "Last seen heading north for Idaho."

—

All my running, all my joking. I see now that I'd been trying to forget something.

Six weeks earlier, in late May, we went to Utah with a group of our friends and their kids for a warm-up rafting trip on the San Juan River. It was an easy, five-day run with only a few moderate Class III rapids, all of which you could portage on foot. We'd floated it half a dozen times since the girls were babies. I'd held them in my arms on the raft while they napped, changed diapers on the sandy tent floor, and nursed them in their lifejackets.

This spring, though, the San Juan was swollen with snowmelt, running higher and faster than we'd ever seen it—an express train of runoff funneling out of the San Juan Mountains in Colorado before joining the Animas and La Plata Rivers and roiling downstream with demonic furor. At the boat launch, I watched a log hurtle by and disappear around a willowy bend, carried swiftly by the root-beer brown river.

It was stupid from the start, given how high and fast the water was, to take my paddle board. But I'd brought it from Santa Fe and blown it up, and it would be a nuisance and a hazard to strap it to the raft or tow it through rapids. I was stubborn, too: for so many years, I'd had to hold the girls on the raft. Now they were finally big enough to sit on their own and move around the boat on sturdy legs, and I was free to jump ship.

Within minutes of launching, I realized I'd made a mistake. The current swelled beneath my board with a muscular, almost animalistic insistence. There were no eddies; all the usual pools of slack water along the shore were washed out by high water. I stood up once and nearly tumbled in.

Time blurred with the rapids, and with their passing arose the feeling that we were being carried somewhere beyond our control and all we could do was hold on. I couldn't hear my friends in front calling to me, I could only see as we rounded a bend that an inconsequential riffle I remembered from years past was now an actual rapid. Foaming waves churned over submerged rocks, and the lip of whitewater curled into itself in endless exact repetition—a pattern formed by invisible forces. A funny thing happens when you focus on a point downstream: you are studying it, and then, in almost the same moment, you are upon it. In an instant, the anticipation of the hazard becomes the hazard itself.

The waves folded over me like an envelope licked shut.

Trapped, I fought to swim to the surface, but the water kept pressing me deeper. The water was white and roiling and, even through my closed eyes, I could see its brightness surrounding me, churning on top of me. It was like being inside a washing machine. Everyone always says that about rapids, but it's true. It really is like that, though the water was brown as cola and, when it doubled back on itself, dark and sinister as seaweed. Still, there was a quality of whiteness under the water that surprised me. I remember being surprised. About so many things. That it was white, and that I was still underwater. I had to swim to the light, I knew this, but I could not tell which was up, like a pilot lost in a storm. What if I swam the wrong way?

I thought I might die.

I thought this might be the way I died.

The river pushed me deeper, but I pushed back, harder, against it. The sensation was one of will and supreme physical effort. The San Juan was making me fight. I pulled and yanked my head, thrashing, toward the surface that I sensed hidden behind my eyes.

Then, at last, I popped out.

My board was very far away. Steve and our raft were very far away. Both were behind me, upstream.

"Help!" I called to him. "Help me!" I had swallowed a lot of water, and my voice scratched my throat.

"Swim toward your board!" Steve yelled.

I was so disoriented it took me a year, it seemed, for my brain to register what I'd been taught to do: float with my feet pointed downstream, above the water. I rolled onto my back. Now that I was floating, this was what I would do forever, because it meant I was safe.

But no. That was not all I had to do.

"Swim to your board!" Steve yelled again.

"No!" I screamed. "Help me!"

I wanted him to scoop me up. Why wasn't he rowing faster to get me? We were doing it again. That thing we did on rivers. Fighting for control. Why did I think someone would ever win?

I flipped onto my belly and front-crawled for shore, sliding downstream with every stroke. Finally, I was there. Grabbed a willow branch and heaved myself onto a rock like a seal, panting.

I could see our raft on the shore just upstream. Steve was rescuing my board and pulling it onto the boat, but then he shot past me, his hand in the air, pointing downriver. A second raft swerved close, and a friend called out, "Are you okay?" but then he, too, was gone.

"Don't leave me!" the crazed woman who was me shrieked again. "Wait!"

The last boat in our group came up behind me, my friend Win rowing fast, trying to get to shore. "I'll pick you up in the next eddy!" he called. The river was so big and thick and boiling with those black waves, but the brushy, snakey bank was no better. I got to my feet and raced down the bank to where Win was waiting. He rowed me to Steve, and I flopped aboard our raft. I clung to the girls as they stroked my legs and soothed me, asking over and over, "Are you afraid of the river now, Mama?"

When we finally found a camp, it was after six and the children were whimpering from hunger. We'd been on the river for five hours without stopping and had covered thirty-two miles. We joked that we'd paddled an ultramarathon, but no one felt like laughing.

Alone in our tent, Steve and I bickered. I wanted him to say, "I was worried," and, "I'm so glad you're okay," but instead he said, "I knew you were fine the whole time."

"How could you know?" I asked. "I was pushed under. It felt like forever."

"It was only a few seconds, and then I saw your head. I knew you were okay."

I could tell by the tone of his voice, pinched and defensive, that he would fight me on this fact until he won or I gave up, and that even if I could convey to him the black menacing waves on the surface and the ice-blue light beneath and the fury of the river pressing down on me, he wouldn't concede my fear. He couldn't. Because that would mean he was scared, too.

In the morning, I woke before everyone else and crept out of camp, picking up each flip-flopped foot and setting it down gently in the sand so as not to wake anyone. The river had come down five feet. Our rafts, which had been floating the night before, rocked gently in the sticky mud at the water's edge. I stared at the current, trying to observe its slackening. Large, dark shapes floated downstream, looking from a distance like animals—dead elephants, horses, rattlesnakes—but when they reached me, I saw they were stumps and sticks washed out of upstream arroyos.

Across the river, tamarisk grew thick on the shore, and the canyon walls shot up, 800 feet of blocky, striated limestone. My body felt like running. I missed it. I always miss it on rivers, where you have to give yourself over to the canyon's rugged walls and jumbles of rocks, devoid of trails in or out. I knew this forced rest was good for me, though. It reminded me that I wasn't in charge; the river was.

I followed a faint trail upstream, hopping saltbush and prickly pear cacti until the path petered out in a pile of limestone boulders sent clattering from the cliff walls who knows how many thousands of years ago. I couldn't run, so I did the next best thing. I sat.

I closed my eyes and breathed and tried not to think about rivers, why I was having such a hard time with them lately, and with Steve. Flow had been replaced by fear. Did I still even *like* rivers? It had been so long since they were simple for us, since *we* were simple. I missed the ease and fluidity of how we used to be.

There's a moment in every meditation when I feel myself take my first real breath, a deep inhalation that goes all the way into my stomach and comes all the way out, and the tension in my throat and chest dissolves. A notion appeared on the horizon of my mind and drifted overhead: I *did* love rivers. I had *always* loved rivers. I breathed this thought in and then out, relinquishing it to the sky. Then I got up and walked back to camp, where Steve greeted me with a cup of coffee.

The river was docile now, and we floated the final days without incident. We camped on bright beaches, slept deeply, from exhaustion or relief, and woke to heavy dew on our sleeping bags. We explored side canyons of gray limestone, flat and smooth as a floor, polished to a high gleam, and found murky pools squirming with tadpoles, where the children stamped and wallowed in the muck, shrieking with glee. My friend Kate flew a kite.

We were in time with the river at last, no longer pushing against the current but trusting ourselves to move with it. I'd forgotten that it takes time and that some rivers take more time than others. But all it takes is time. That's all it's ever taken.

At the take-out, a strange mix of jubilation and chagrin came over us, as though we'd gotten away with something, but barely. Our near-miss hung like a shadow, a stroke of luck that maybe we didn't all the way deserve.

In the days after, we tried to make sense of the trip. The weather, we agreed, was perfect, but the river had been hard on us—impassive, unrelenting, determined to teach us a lesson we still needed to learn: be vigilant, don't be complacent. And at the same time: let go. Like the rocks that tumble from canyon walls, unhooking themselves from the knitted earth and surrendering to the long fall.

It was three weeks later that I went looking for books for the Salmon, and I'm sure I was thinking about the San Juan just a little when I bought *The Summer He Didn't Die*. Because I hadn't died, not yet, though I felt in a way that the once-fearless girl in me had.

6. IDAHO

On June 23rd, the first full day of summer, the Middle Fork boat launch at Boundary Creek, Idaho, is mobbed with trucks and trailers and people unloading rafts and brightly colored dry bags filled with gear and enough food and water for a week in the wilderness. The embankment is so steep rafts have to be lowered by winch down a splintery wooden ramp. Below, the narrow beach is buried in rafts, six deep, lashed one to the next so they're not swept away.

Stuck to a post beside the door of the small ranger station is the river gauge. It resembles a giant yardstick, the kind you use to measure snowfall or the sad, slow progress of a school fundraiser. The Middle Fork of the Salmon is measured by how many feet above its bank the river flows, rather than the standard measurement of cubic feet per second. A height of two feet is considered rocky and impassable; five feet qualifies as high water; six is hazardous. There's a narrow window between too little water on the Middle Fork and too much. Judging from the yardstick, we're in it: the line is slashed at three feet. As is typical for late June, the river is coming down from peak snowmelt runoff and, though it's still tricky, technical, and riddled with exposed rocks, it's theoretically runnable.

Our group consists of eight boats and twenty-two people. We know four of them: our two friends, Rob and Amy, and their two teenage kids. I've known Rob for fifteen years, since we worked together at an outdoor magazine in Santa Fe. He and Amy have been our river mentors since our girls were babies, showing us how to safely raft with humans so tiny they didn't yet talk or walk and how not to lose our minds, at least not all the way. The rest of our group on the Middle Fork are friends of Amy's brother, the trip leader, and friends of his friends, a loose spiral of connections radiating outward from the center. There's a small but mighty contingent of men in their early sixties through mid-seventies, seasoned Middle Fork boatmen who've run the river twelve times among them and know every rapid at every level.

While we wait for our turn to launch, a river ranger calls us over to a picnic table in the shade for a safety talk. He runs through emergency scenarios and camping rules. "Don't burn trash in the campfire," he tells us. "Especially plastic. It releases toxins into the air."

The group nods dutifully. I wrinkle my nose and look at Steve, who's eating a turkey sandwich, plastic wrap balled in his fist. *As if we'd ever burn trash*, his indignant look says.

I roll my eyes. *As if.*

At last, the ramp is clear, and it's our turn to send our boats over the cliff edge and down the steep ramp. The last thing I do is take a picture of our blue raft against the rickety, sun-faded wood; my legs cast a long, ungainly shadow over the photograph. Then I tuck my phone into the pocket of my life jacket and let the momentum of the day carry me down the path to the river.

I've never flipped in a raft before.

I know how to see the "V" in the current at the top of a rapid, signaling the easiest entry, and how to ride the tongue of a wave all the way to the bottom. I know how to roll an overturned kayak and how to swim out from under it. I know how to keep my toes pointed downstream so my feet don't become entrapped. And I know—on rivers, as in life—how to look where I want to go, not where I don't.

But I don't know how to fall out of a raft. Not on the Middle Fork of the Salmon River, not now, not anywhere.

Less than ten minutes after we launch from the boat ramp, we are wrapped around the rock. It sticks out of the water like the prow of a sinking ship, big and sharp and gray. I am stranded high on the port side of our raft, and the rock is starboard, but we are not spinning off of it like Steve is so sure we will. Instead the current is pushing us harder against it.

I hold on for what feels like a year but might be one second, and then the raft is over all the way, and I'm dangling inches from swirling river.

Then I'm in.

I'm in.

"I'm in!"

I am thinking this and yelling it at the same time.

The water is only a foot deep, two at most, but I can't stand up for fear of my feet becoming entrapped. Instead, I drag on the bottom, hitting rocks and jostling off them. Frantically, I scan the river. The upside-down raft floats on, leaving us. Steve is a head bobbing in the water far in front of me.

On my back. Legs, bottom, elbows bouncing over boulders. All I can think about: rocks.

Then: shore. Get to shore.

I spin onto my stomach. Right away, I can tell something is wrong. My left knee is flopping, loose, like wobbly chicken fat jostling in its joint, side to side, up and down. No pain, just the terrible jiggling. The water makes it worse. I doggy-paddle toward the left shore, ten feet away, maybe twenty. The raft and my people disappear ahead of me around a bend in the river.

I let the current push me toward shore. In the shallowest water along the edge, I try to climb up onto the bank, but my knee feels as though it has been scooped out on the inside. I pull myself, soaked and floppy, onto a half-submerged rock using only my arms. My left knee swivels in its socket. Nothing remains to keep it upright, and I know then that our trip is over and we will be walking out.

But that's not what happens.

7. STORIES

We are made up of stories. The stories are not entirely made up, rather clarified by time and telling, reduced again and again until only the essential is left. As a very young girl, my mother ate deadly nightshade in a neighbor's garden and survived. She quit college to marry at twenty-one and later paid a farmer to drive her to the coed university an hour away because the college where she lived with her husband did not allow women. If she had regrets, they weren't worth talking about.

The stories are told aloud and retold or written in notebooks with spiral bindings. They live in our memories and on our computers, in the cloud and in our minds. They live in photographs and pictures drawn on paper, as forgotten conversations, as notes we write, and as letters in the bottom of a shoebox.

They live in our bodies as movement. In our muscles and blood and cells, fascia, organs, and feet, in our slumbering minds. When our limbs twitch in our sleep, our feet tripping over dream-rocks, these are stories, too.

Some stories we tell over and over until they become well-worn; they return to us again and again, unbidden but not unwelcome, bearers of messages we have yet to decode, reminders that time is a folded accordion with infinite creases. Others we rarely tell, not because we don't remember them, but because we worry that reconstructing them will alter them for good.

The stories change over time. Sometimes not much time. They become refined, they shift to reveal new lessons, morals. The tone changes, too, from one of tragedy to triumph, or the other way around. We talk ourselves into our stories. This is how we learn to live with what happened.

Stories reveal our true natures, and we shape the stories to our nature, tease out the moments that encapsulate something singular, that we might have otherwise missed. Steve, pensively studying the Rice Krispies box one morning at breakfast: "I don't think I ever noticed they were *rice* elves."

All stories are filled with invisible things, traces of the time and place in which they are told: pine needles and rocks, a girl's loneliness, swimming, ice cream cones after dinner, the light through a curtain when I wake at dawn to write lines I dreamed in my sleep. You can't see these shadows, but they're here.

Likewise, when you read a story or hear it told, you fill it with your own hidden ingredients: your mother's voice calling you for dinner, the room above a lake where you turn these pages. In this way, every story about the past is also the story of now, just as it already contains the future. A story's landscape is continuously shifting, gathering more particles as it goes, remaking itself, the way a body does.

Stories, by definition, are a flawed facsimile. They create a gap, a layer between reality and our idea of it; what we are telling is the memory of the moment rather than the moment. Stories obscure reality even as they attempt to express it; they create distance even as they attempt to bring us closer. They fail at the very function they are meant to fulfill.

That's the problem with stories.

Of course we tell them anyway.

—

The notebook I kept that week on the Middle Fork is just like the others I've used for almost two decades: slim, with a soft binding and one hundred lined pages. The cover is cherry red. When I dig it out from the cardboard peach boxes where I store them in deliberate disarray, there's nothing to identify what's inside, except for a small smudge of dried mud on the back. It's the early weeks of a global pandemic; we are homebound, the streets deserted, the whole world shut. The words inside are whispers from another time. Will it tell the story I remember or a different one?

Flipping through the pages, I can see that the trip had fractured into pieces. There is not one account but two: the trip in my memory and the one in my notebook. Both are imperfect sketches, glaring omissions of fact mingled with strange, almost surreal tangents, the ghost outline of an accident and its aftermath. If I patch them together, will I have a complete picture? Can I close the gap between the reality of what had happened and my rendition of it, to see below the story to its essence, what in Zen is called *true nature*?

It had been too soon, and too painful, to tell the whole story of Idaho in a straight line while I was on the river. I can see this in my notebook. The story surfaces in patchwork, out of order, playing leapfrog with itself—less an accounting of facts than a study of mind and memory. I'd told it to myself in bits and pieces, backward, parsing the details in a strange, buckled chronology that bore little resemblance to real time. The fragments, jotted hastily in crooked handwriting, defy a neat narrative. Instead they seem to offer something far stranger, and just as accidental: an unfiltered expression of trauma, rather than an interpretation of it.

My fall from the raft was a break in the timeline—a sharp fracture between before and after. The start of one thing and the end of something else.

—

> *In the painful or unreal parts I write in third person
> because she is the girl who did that growing up—made up
> elaborate stories about other people and their frights so
> she could get out of her body and into her imagination.*

In the red notebook, certain details emerge as essential.

She is flipped out of the raft at mile 1.5. The Middle Fork is one hundred miles long. On the first evening after the accident, she lies in the tent her husband has pitched for them in a charred moonscape of a camp and tries not to cry. Her husband is fly-fishing. Her knee and shin have swollen into a long cylindrical balloon, the kind

she used to get as a girl at the shoe store when her mother bought
her new sneakers.

> *The girl knows how to run. It is as simple as anything. She*
> *has known for almost as long as she could walk. Running*
> *is not the complicated part. What she carries is.*

She can't tell which is worse, the fear in her mind or the pain in
her leg.

Feeling woozy, she lifts herself up on one elbow, keeps writing:

> *Sometimes you want to go nowhere specific. You just want*
> *to explore. You just want to move. You go out on your*
> *three-speed bike after dinner when the light is fading, and*
> *you ride. This is how you learn a new place, wandering,*
> *with no particular destination.*
>
> *Sometimes you get lost, and your mother comes out in*
> *the wood-paneled Oldsmobile station wagon to find you*
> *and herd you home. "Oh there you are!" she says in her*
> *bright voice, hiding her worry. She was always so good at*
> *that. There's not a chance you will get in the car with her.*
> *You're going to ride home. This is who you are and have*
> *always been.*
>
> *Why this comes to mind here, in an Idaho river canyon,*
> *she has no idea. Maybe she is tired of going in a straight*
> *line. Maybe deep down she has wanted this but didn't*
> *know it. Not this exactly but some version of it. The chance*
> *to rest and swirl around a bit, neither forward nor back, to*
> *let go of the part of her that wants only to move ahead in*
> *one direction, relentlessly.*

8. RIVER OF NO RETURN

I am collected on the shore and ferried downstream to Steve and our overturned raft on the opposite bank. My leg thuds with a long dull ache, as though I'm swathed in shock, coddled by it. Questions are posed and answered: No, I didn't hit my knee on anything I could remember. Yes, I bumped my whole body. No, my head is fine.

When I try to reconstruct what happened next, I find that I can't. I can't remember Steve pulling me to his wet and shivering body, though surely he did. I can't remember being wrapped in a fleece jacket, though surely I was. I can't remember crying, though surely I did.

I remember thinking: Now what?

A woman bent over me, saying maybe I dislocated my knee. That had happened to her recently and it had swollen terribly, but later it went back into place on its own and she was fine!

I remember liking that idea. Much more than having torn my ACL and all the ligaments in my knee and needing surgery, which is what the runner in me feared most.

The group huddled together, reviewing options. The options were confusing. The math did not make sense. We were less than two miles into our hundred-mile trip. We had ninety-eight rapids and ninety-eight miles to go. This would take us six days. Or we could walk upstream two miles, bashing through trees and brush along the riverbank with one wrecked leg. This might take five hours. We would have to pull our raft to shore, stash it with all our gear, and hope it would still be there when we came back for it at an unknown later time.

There were so many variables.

Don't push the river.

Injured, I was a liability to the rest of the group, so we all had to agree.

I could tell Steve wanted to go on, did not want to leave the river or the boat. Who knew when we could come back?

Inventory was taken. Our paltry first aid kit consisted of an Ace bandage, some Advil, strong pain meds, and the emergency satellite beacon Steve and I had brought.

More questions, this time about my toes. Could I feel them? That's a good sign. More wriggling.

It was agreed. We would keep going.

At least until tomorrow, when we would pass the first airstrip, at Indian Creek.

(Forgotten: Did I agree?)

I would ride aboard a different raft, a cataraft with twin rubber pontoons that made it more stable than our traditional oar raft. The captain's name was Frank. He was in his late fifties or early sixties, with graying hair, and had rafted the Middle Fork so many times he'd lost count. "At least a dozen," he said. "I'll get you down safely."

The important thing was that I couldn't fall out again. I had to stay in the boat. No matter what.

I was lifted into Frank's boat. His wife, Lisa, was there. She had perky, dyed blonde hair, a hot pink life jacket, and a New Jersey accent. Frank's oars made a soft gurgling sound as we pulled from shore and back into the river that made me feel, momentarily, unafraid.

What I remember are the butterflies that flitted around the raft as Frank rowed, yellow and black monarchs flouncing the air with delicate wings, and Lisa, clutching my hand, telling me they were the spirits of protectors, people we loved from our last lives guarding us as we floated downstream.

—

Slowly, after a shock, the world comes back into focus.

Camp that night was an ash pile left over from a recent forest fire. I'd been expecting the burned areas to look stark and grim, but they were just as striking as the healthy ponderosa pines along both banks. Trees stuck out of the earth, charred and pointy, leaning at precarious angles like half-torched matchsticks marching up mountainsides. You could see so much farther through the scorched forest—landscapes otherwise hidden to the human eye, revealed. The burns were beautiful because they were natural.

Steve and Rob heaved me up from the raft to a high, flat place, my arms slung around theirs and theirs around me. They set me down in the dust with my notebook while they and everyone else busied themselves setting up tents.

I pinched my toes to check for feeling. They'd ballooned up, fat and stubby like miniature hot dogs—diminutive versions of my humongous, grotesque knee. Steve went fishing, caught a few. People ate dinner out of plastic bowls and drank cheap canned beer, and someone played the guitar, like it was any other night on any other river.

I sat in the dirt taking notes in a messy scrawl. *Frank rides a recumbent bicycle. Lisa pronounces water "warter." I fell out of the raft when it tipped on a rock. I want to go home.*

Time ran together. It was night but not dark yet because it was Idaho at the summer solstice, and I needed to sleep but couldn't. My leg was a wad of stiffness. In the tent, I had to lie on my back and not move, with my knee propped up on my dry bag to keep the swelling down. Steve lay beside me. We were fighting but trying not to be heard through the thin nylon walls.

It was our same argument about control, only in reverse this time. Why hadn't he pulled us off the rock? Why hadn't he been more assertive? Why hadn't I? Why hadn't I fallen out of the boat the right way? Hard, blaming words hissed back and forth, compounded by shock and fatigue. The adrenaline had worn off, and my knee pulsed with a deep thumping ache. I lay awake for a long time, waiting for something—an apology, remorse, mine and his—but soon Steve was snoring, and I must have fallen asleep eventually, too, because when I opened my eyes, I was alone in the tent, and the light outside was gray and thin: dawn.

I'd dreamed that my leg was fine and had healed in the night. I could walk again. The dream was so vivid it seemed real, but when I tried to roll over, my knee throbbed, and I knew it wasn't true, and I felt like crying.

I peered through the tent flap. Steve was in the camp kitchen. All around us the trees were blackened matchstick charred into spears by the last fire.

It was pretty, the torched forest that was slowly coming back to life, when you looked at it in a certain way.

Hadn't I wanted to know what that felt like? To become the fire?

9. NOT KNOWING

All our usual river trip routines evaporated, replaced by new ones. I couldn't help load the rafts or take down the tents. I couldn't walk up the shore and around the bend or run the trail along the river. I had to stay where I was put.

When I needed to pee, Steve set me down on a rock and I wriggled my nylon river shorts below my hips and urinated right in the dirt. It might have looked like I was sitting on a rock, but really I was peeing, in front of everyone, while they turned their heads discreetly to give me privacy. Somehow this was the most humiliating part, worse even than the little spray of urine that hit the ground and splashed up onto my ankles—that everyone had to stop what they were doing to look away.

Breakfast was brought to me each morning, a cup of coffee, black, and a hastily assembled egg burrito with hash browns spilling out the side. I sat with my plate balanced poorly on my lap, my notebook on my thigh, trying to write and eat at the same time. I felt foolish and self-conscious about falling from the boat and getting hurt and putting a damper on the trip for the others, and my embarrassment became a kind of self-inflicted estrangement. Steve and I had an unspoken rule when we traveled with friends into the backcountry: always be helpful, organized, and keep your shit together. Never be the problem on a trip. Now I was.

> There are too many factors to think about. My knee,
> my dead phone that fell in the river, my marriage,
> my knee, my running, that I can't think about
> any of them.
>
> I am right here on this log, not knowing.

—

There's a famous Zen koan in which one monk meets another while walking along a trail and asks him where he's going. "I'm on a pilgrimage," the traveling monk answers. "What's that?" the other monk asks. When the traveler replies, "I don't know," the first monk looks at him sagely, as though he's uttered a profound truth, and says, "Not knowing is most intimate." Upon hearing these words, the pilgrim is said to have experienced a great awakening.

In Zen, not knowing is considered a form of wisdom. Being willing to accept uncertainty brings you closer to the truth of life. When you no longer hold fast to fixed ideas or outcomes, to what you want to happen, you see more clearly what is happening.

Koans embody the truth of not-knowing. These ancient Zen tales, often numbered as "cases," will never tell you what to do or think. Rather, they demonstrate teachings, through animals and objects and strange scenarios and old masters whose utterances are so deliciously cryptic you feel like you're reading the words backward while standing on your head. Even the commentaries that follow the cases, intended to elucidate the deeper truth, are as enigmatic as the stories themselves.

Ambiguity is inherently uncomfortable. It's human nature to want to know how things will turn out—a prehistoric survival instinct hardwired into us from the days when our ancestors had to outsmart mastodons and forage for food. I'd taken a crash course in not-knowing when my father died, quickly, of a cancer no one saw coming. Motherhood, too, is a protracted exercise in instability. Then again, when you look closely, you see that all of life is this way—we just do a very good job pretending otherwise, and life, for a time, lets us.

In a culture that demands and rewards certainty and guarantees, not-knowing is an outlier position. It's not the same, though, as willful ignorance or passive ambivalence, nor is it contraindicative of competence. In fact, like all true Zen paradoxes, not-knowing is considered a deep form of knowing, an elevated state of consciousness, arguably even a form of mastery. It's the ability to tap into instinct and intuition. "Knowing not-knowing," Zen Master Dogen called it.

Running long distances had helped boost my tolerance for uncertainty. You could train well and prepare for all sorts of challenging conditions, but over the course of thirty miles or sixty, unanticipated problems were always bound to arise. How you dealt with them determined your success as much as, or even more than, how hard you trained.

My writing, too, flowed more easily from don't-know mind. If I went into a story or assignment with a preconceived idea of what would happen, or worse, a meticulous outline, I'd get stuck even before I began. Over time, I learned to write not to make something happen, but to find out what happens—to write my way into knowing.

Still, sometimes not-knowing felt like playing hide-and-seek in a pitch-black basement, hands outstretched, feeling for the soft contours of familiar bodies without smashing into the furniture— disorienting and a little terrifying. I'd written "not knowing is the most important thing" on a scrap of paper and taped it above my writing desk for encouragement. When I looked at these words, I could remember that I preferred not knowing to mapping out a life and hoping very much to keep on the trails but never being able to, not all the way, forever.

—

Frank was graceful and fluid on the oars. He seemed to need to take fewer strokes than anyone else and had mastered the precise formula of expending exactly the right effort to steer us safely through obstacles: one sedate pull on the left oar would spin us perfectly to the left, skirting holes and finding the smoothest line over ledges and into rapids.

I sat in the stern, on a platform straddling the two pontoons, behind Lisa, my left leg stretched out and propped up on a dry bag. My knee was so stiff and engorged I couldn't bend it; I had to pick it up and move it manually, like a small log.

Frank had salt-and-pepper hair, a friendly, bumbling manner, and skinny legs that stuck out beneath his life jacket. He worked in nuclear waste transfer in Twin Falls and taught motorcycle lessons for fun on the side. The oldest of the Idaho river rats, Bob, who was seventy-five, declared Frank the best boatman on the river.

"There's our patient!" Frank exclaimed the second morning, after Steve carried me to the raft. His tone was one of pure delight, as though he'd never been so happy in all his life to have an unexpected and injured passenger on board.

"I'm scared to stay on," I blurted out.

"There's nothing harder than that first day," Frank said, smiling reassuringly beneath the brim of his floppy sun hat. "I know these rapids, and there's nothing that worries me, so you can take that worry right off the list." If he was bullshitting me, I wanted nothing more than to believe him. But I'd seen the river map, littered with hash marks signifying the dozens of major rapids that awaited us.

I could tell we were approaching a rapid when Frank rose silently from his seat and scanned the horizon line on the river, picking his entry. The old-timers dubbed this move the Prairie Dog, after the rodents that popped their furry heads out of holes to look for predators. There was too much to say, and nothing I could say would improve our chances, so I sat as still as possible, gripping a blue lash strap with one hand and Lisa's hand with the other. "Honey," she'd say at the top of every rapid, squeezing my hand.

If it was awkward that I was riding with Frank and not my own husband, Frank was too polite to mention it. After the first night, no one talked about the accident or Steve's rowing or my falling or the fact that we might pose a risk to ourselves and the group or, worse, that maybe we weren't cut out for big rivers. Steve and I weren't talking much, either. We were both still trying to process what had happened, focused on getting downstream safely and on behaving and on not being the people on the trip who cause more problems by bickering.

Frank's cataraft was steadier than our thirteen-foot oar boat, less prone to flipping, and therefore my safest option, but this meant Steve had to navigate the river solo. When I saw him ahead of us, bucking through another hydraulic in our bright blue raft, which looked dinky and toylike against the frothing river, my shame and anger dissolved, chiseled down to dust by the clear, bright water and the jagged boulders and, most of all, an overwhelming love for Steve. In those moments, I forgot my grief for my leg and my frustration that he hadn't rowed us off the rock. All I wanted was for Steve to get through safely.

Each time we cleared a rapid, Frank set his oars down to rest a minute, always without fanfare. At most he might utter, "Well, that got my heart going," or, "I thought that rock had my name written all over it," even though he never looked like he was sweating it. If a rock forced him to take a stroke one way or the other, he'd chide it gently: "You rascal!"

Most of the time, Frank was quiet, gazing at the shore approvingly and occasionally pointing out magnificent, gnarled ponderosa pines and bald eagles, or looking for bighorn sheep. "I want to see some sheep," he'd murmur. "I think we're gonna see some sheep."

10. ONE RAPID AT A TIME

So it's happened. I've gotten hurt in the wilderness. I've seen that it can happen, of course it can, and now it's happened to me. A rite of passage, it was only a matter of time. Maybe I just dislocated my knee. I didn't hear a pop.

Once I'd settled on this story, I had to go over it in my head, reviewing it for loopholes, logic problems. I needed to make sure it held water. If it did, I could believe it, and if I could believe it, I could hold out the gauziest shred of hope for a good outcome.

In order to do this, I had to suspend disbelief. I had to ignore the pain, and to ignore the pain, I had to identify its source and avoid it at all costs. Then I could pretend it wasn't so bad. I could keep going. I could stay on the river with Steve even though I was afraid and angry and desperately wanted to go home.

Only once did I allow myself to wonder. Alone in the tent, I grazed the ground with my toe. A spear of agony shot through my knee all the way to my teeth. The idea rose, unbidden: maybe it's broken.

But no. Don't follow that thought. Don't say it out loud. Don't get ahead of yourself. Focus instead on what has to be done: Face each rapid as it comes, one at a time. Stay in the boat.

I could see that this would have to become my practice for the coming days: a ruthless, single-minded focus in which I could not think about the worries crowding in, all the scenarios I couldn't control, but instead must concentrate on what was right in front of me. It was strangely clarifying, and the tiniest bit calming.

I knew from meditation that this was what you were supposed to try to do. Just breathe this breath and then the next, be in this moment and then the next, but there were always so many distractions, so many happy, pleasing distractions to lead you astray and into your imagination or to the next very good moment unfolding in your life.

Injured and immobilized in the middle of the wilderness, though, there were fewer good things unfolding—and no place to go but right where I was.

We were coming up on Indian Creek airstrip at river mile twenty-one. The night before, I'd texted my mother on our emergency satellite beacon. I HURT MY LEG, BUT I'M OKAY. All I had to do was send her my location and ask her to arrange for a flight, and within hours a bush plane with a lawnmower engine would buzz the canyon to scoop me up. If I didn't leave now, I only had one more chance—the Flying B guest ranch thirty miles, and two days, downstream.

Indian Creek came into view on a grassy bench above the river; an orange windsock dangled from its post above the landing strip. But I'd already made up my mind.

> Decided to go on, past Indian Creek airstrip. Knee
> still swollen and cannot bear weight. So dirty. Wear-
> ing same clothes every day, too hard to change them.
> Filthy, streaked sunglasses. Half a pound of sand in my
> sleeping bag.

Below that, in my red notebook, I'd copied a line from Joy Williams: "Cherish anything that wakes you up, even for a moment." And then:

> Am I awake in this canyon?
> Yes. Awake but compromised.
> Purely enduring. Just trying to get downstream.
> I want to go home.
> I want to be awake.

Reading this years later, I wish I could go back and tell myself, *It's okay. It will all be okay. You want Steve to hold you. Hold him instead.*

In the morning at Little Soldier Camp, the sky was blue and I sat in plumes of drifting campfire ash. Someone tossed a bacon package into the flames, filling the air with the rancid odor of burning plastic and pork grease. Despite, or perhaps because of, the ranger's admonitions, the Idaho crew had taken to burning trash with wild and gleeful abandon. Everything went into the fire: soda cans, plastic bags, candy wrappers, tinfoil, paper plates, leftover food scraps. This reduced to nearly nil both the amount of trash we had to haul downstream and the dishes that had to be washed—a sly, if completely verboten, strategy. Their disobedience was so flagrant, it was almost funny. "Idaho-style," Steve nicknamed it; later, after we'd made it down and out of the canyon, it would become our inside joke, code for all manner of dubious river behavior.

A yellow bush plane clamored overhead, bisecting the river with its shiny, mustard wings. The slow current along the shore as it whorled over the stony beach sounded like a persistent, soft, human murmuring. Somebody telling a secret.

—

When I turned forty, in 2011, Steve and I went on a raft trip through the Grand Canyon. Like the Middle Fork, the Grand—as it's known—is a seminal whitewater rite of passage. Private permits are nearly impossible to come by—we had friends who'd waited a decade or more for their name to be drawn—and the water is so big and so committing that we signed up for a commercial trip. The girls were one and three, and my mother flew out to Santa Fe to babysit. Most trips through the full Canyon require two or three weeks, but we only had one, so we planned to leave the group and hike out from Phantom Ranch, midway through.

Because we had guides, Steve and I didn't have to make decisions or plan meals or pack food, load boats or choose where to camp. All we had to do was follow instructions. It felt like a true vacation, all the very best parts of being on a river without any of the logistical stress. Our first morning in camp, we slept so late the guides had to wake us. It was the sleep of the dead, of delirium. Our fatigue was so complete, we'd forgotten we were tired.

Because we were the youngest guests on the trip by twenty years, the guides agreed to let us paddle an inflatable double kayak through the smaller rapids. "It's just like a tandem bike," Steve told me, grinning slyly, as we climbed in for the first time. We had a joke that we were never, ever to ride a tandem bicycle together. It would be a recipe for disaster, or divorce.

In our tiny rubber boat in the Grand Canyon, though, we made a thrillingly good team. There was so much water and the rapids were so huge we didn't have to look for rocks. We didn't have to make any decisions. We just had to follow our guides' line and keep the inflatable ducky straight and paddle hard in unison, bucking and bouncing through the waves to the calm water below. The other guests watched from the guides' wooden dories, their mouths widened in excitement and alarm, waiting for us to flip, maybe even secretly hoping we would, for the vicarious thrill of it. At the bottom of each rapid, Steve and I threw high fives and whooped with laughter and adrenaline, as surprised as the others that we were still upright. We didn't capsize once that week.

I was falling in love again—with the water and the way it moved so steadily on its way to places I couldn't name or see, with our brief, newfound freedom, with my husband. New parenthood is one very long game of tag. *I'll take the babies while you work, you take the babies while I run. One handoff after another: Here, I'm going skiing. When you come back, I'll write. Tag, you're it.* This is the way it has to be for both parties to stay sane, but it has an insidious way of turning spouses into strangers. Now at last I had Steve back again.

I didn't want the trip to end, and when Steve suggested I stay on and float another seven days through the Lower Canyon, while he drove back to Santa Fe to spell my mother, I wanted so badly to say yes. I walked up to the pay phone at Phantom Ranch to call home and tell Mom he'd be coming back as planned and I was going to keep going, but even before my mother picked up, I knew I wouldn't stay. It was Steve I wanted to be with—more than the canyon, more than the river.

—

Flying B Ranch, mile sixty-six, was the last grass airstrip before the canyon choked in on itself, below which there was no getting in or out except by raft.

The night before, at Hospital Bar camp, a cobbly beach at mile fifty-three (named for a medical tent located here during the gold rush—sadly, long gone), Steve and Rob lugged me 300 yards upstream to a natural hot spring pool at the river's edge. It took almost an hour roundtrip, and by the time we got back to our tent, my shoulders felt like they were about to rip straight out of their sockets, but it was worth it—soaking my swollen, buoyant leg in warm water with the rest of the group, pretending for a little while that nothing had happened.

In the morning, we all agreed that we'd land the rafts at Flying B and walk up to the ranch store and buy ice cream sandwiches and maybe look into a flight out. No one was pressuring me to leave, but I knew this would be my last chance to cut my trip short and get to a doctor. The river widened lazily in the final straightaway before the ranch and overhead, we heard the buzz of a bush plane, coming in for a landing. The timing was uncanny: Had my stepfather, worried for my safety, called for an evacuation? He would do that. Emergencies were his specialty. He never panicked. He took action: whatever needed to be done, he did it. There was no one you wanted more in a crisis than Ron.

When I saw the plane looping languidly over the river—its dark body an affront to the blue sky, like a vulture circling—I knew I didn't want to go. I didn't want to leave Steve or the group or Frank or Lisa. I didn't want to be saved. I wanted to save myself, the way I had when I'd gotten lost on my bicycle as a girl.

Steve dropped me over his shoulders and and walked up to the ranch; the screen door slammed behind us. Inside was cool and dim—a creaky-floored outpost in the middle of the wilderness. You could mail postcards and buy beer. You could leave notes on a bulletin board for river runners upstream. We asked the shopkeeper behind the counter about flights. The plane we'd seen was just a sightseeing excursion, he told us. He'd have to call for a charter. It would cost me 200 dollars to fly to the town of Salmon, and then I'd still have to figure out how to get to the clinic in Sun Valley. The soonest I'd get there was the next day.

I looked at Steve and shook my head. I hadn't known I'd been holding my breath until I let it out in a long exhale.

Another raft trip was coming in as we were going out. "What happened to you?" one of the boaters asked, eying the purple leg warmer, soggy and dark as a pelt, that swaddled my fattened knee.

"Flipped on the first day," I said.

"You flying out?" he said.

I shook my head. "No," I said, "I'm going on."

When Steve set me down on the raft, Frank patted the back of my lifejacket. "Glad you didn't leave us," he said. "This is where things get good."

Now the questions were answered. No more wondering. We were committed. There was nowhere to go but down.

—

Staying in the game. Sort of against my better judgment. No waiting overnight at Flying B, alone, not being able to pee or lie down by myself. That would be harder than running Class IV rapids with a busted knee. My instinct says I'm safer here with Steve, sticking together even though my brain and the voice of conformity are telling me it's absurd beyond stupid. Almost anyone else would have gotten out.

—

Just ahead were some of the biggest rapids on the Middle Fork: Marble Creek, Ski Jump, Jackass, Tappan, Tappan Falls, Tappan Two, Haystack, Aparejo, Jack's Creek, Webber. They came so quickly, one upon the next, that they seemed to run together into one long, jumbled chronology.

Plunging over the four-foot drop at Tappan Falls, I surprised myself by hollering "This is fun!" At the bottom, Lisa and I threw high fives. Haystack was more technical: start right of a boulder, move left, then work right again, picking your way through the boulders and cobbles and pillowy rocks and hydraulics. Haystack was an intellectual's rapid, like chess: all strategy and deliberation. Tappan, on the other hand, required more punch, a solid thrusting effort on the oars. We had to keep our momentum. The waves crashed over Frank, splashing Lisa and me. The river glittered beauty and power, swirling onward with endless, surefooted energy.

Anejo caused us only a bit of trouble. Lisa and I weren't expecting the bony wave train riddled with rocks, and toward the bottom, the raft dove into one and stalled. I flew forward, bumping my forehead on the back of Frank's rowing seat. "Holy smokes!" he cried. This was the most agitated I'd seen him, his volume inching up only slightly louder than a toddler's indoor voice.

Jack's Creek was our last rapid of the day, a long series of bends where the river chokes beneath canyon walls and becomes narrower as it wends through a series of constrictions. "Short and straightforward," the guidebook called it.

"That thing's got a sneaky little rock in it; it's got my name on it," Frank said as we approached. "I'll be watching for it." And with a few strokes, we'd cleared it and were through.

When Steve wasn't hauling me around camp or rowing our tiny blue toy boat through the rapids, he was fly-fishing. In the long calm pools between the whitewater, one of our group rowed our boat while Steve stood in the bow, casting for rainbow trout, spooling the long line out in graceful loops. He fished before breakfast and after breakfast, before dinner and after. He must have prepared a meal or two for everyone, as we'd planned, but I have no recollection of what we ate, only the sensation of feeling ashamed and sorry, as though I were ruining a party, while the others moved in careful constellations around me, and Steve pulled speckled, gleaming cutthroat trout from the river and tossed them back.

He seemed utterly unruffled by the turn of events. It was like watching an alien species. How could he stay so calm, so even-keeled, so maddeningly unphased? Steve was a gardener by passion and trade. He planted seeds in the earth and then waited for them to grow. Waiting was Steve's game, and watching. The summer I met him, he grew squash and zucchini as long as his arm. I thought that was how we would live, peaceably turning over new ground each year, never in a hurry, never doubting that good things would bloom.

It was so different from how I'd been raised, which was to keep busy, to always stay in motion like a bundled ball of energy bouncing in a dozen directions at once. We did not wait for things to happen in my family; we made them happen. Here at last was someone with whom I could finally learn to relax.

Of course, in the Murphy's Law of marriage, the very qualities we admire most in someone become the ones that that drive us crazy. I'd fallen in love with Steve's imperturbability, his seemingly interminable patience. On the river, though, they read as passivity, even neglect. Why had he waited to see what the current would do, rather than take one more oar stroke to pull us off the rock?

And almost certainly, Steve would say the same of me. Why could I never settle down, why was I always pushing, why did I always have to be the one to be in control?

> *I am trying not to hate Steve. I am trying to be compassionate. He is sorry and also mortified. The sense of having to prove himself now. Mostly I am not mad. If I can channel compassion, I am not mad.*

In the late afternoon at Parrot Placer camp, mile eighty-six, deep within Impassible Canyon, the light of the setting sun slid slowly up the canyon wall. Frank stood quietly, watching Steve reel in his line. They each studied the water in silence for a few moments. Then Frank spoke in his low, calm voice, but just loud enough for me to hear, "You're having a good run. You're doing well. That upstream rock was just a fluke." I could tell from his approving tone that it was sincere praise and well deserved, and that Steve felt it, too. For a minute I loved my husband as much as I ever had, even more, and I forgot to be angry.

—

In fourteen years together, Steve and I had never had a conventional relationship. Not because we'd planned it or decided this in advance, but because we lived this way. He cooked and ran his own landscaping company, kept us well-fed and sheltered. I had a desk job at a magazine and traveled on assignments. But after the girls were born, our arrangement slowly began to shift. I stayed home with them and wrote on the side, my days consumed by emotional labor: untold hours organizing school and activities, doctor's appointments, family adventures, new shoes for growing feet. Mothers have been doing care labor like this forever, around the clock and with no pay. Some days I felt as if this labor was invisible, worthless, and that I in turn was worthless, lacking economic value and legitimacy.

At the magazine, my job was to make sure my colleagues met their deadlines and, if they didn't, to pester them until they did. Many days that's how motherhood and marriage felt to me, too: like a mid-level managerial position that I performed with lackluster enthusiasm, yielding mediocre results. I hadn't wanted to be anyone's manager or wife—I'd always only wanted to be me, with Steve, and Steve, in his laid-back way, mostly let me. This was his true genius, his deepest appeal, a quietly confident equanimity that was recognizable the moment I met him. He would make no dangerous claims on me, ask for nothing more than I was willing to give. But what if he needed more, and I did, too? Our calculations didn't account for that scenario.

The flip side of freedom is avoidance, and for years we'd been sliding into fixed, unspoken assumptions and interpretations of who we were, separately and together:

I was independent and strong (read, unloving and stubborn).

He was steady and reliable (read, emotionally unavailable).

We'd been storing up these stories about ourselves and each other for so long that we'd started to believe them, and, at the same time, we hated them. Hated them so fiercely it sometimes felt as though we hated each other.

—

The next morning, our last on the Middle Fork. Routines that felt unfamiliar only days before had become ritual. Pore over the whitewater guide, heads bunched, to discuss the biggest hazards, the safest line. Steel ourselves for the rapids ahead. The river, swirling and clear, now almost, already, a memory.

Rubber, Hancock, House Rock rapids. We were in the flow at last, feeling the tug of an ending. And there it was, as we rounded a final bend: a small puff of dust hanging in the air over the far bank. It was moving. Our eyes, accustomed to trees and river and sky and mountains, refocused. It wasn't a trick, it was a truck, rumbling along the dirt road that hugged the far side of the river, towing a raft.

We'd come to the confluence. The Middle Fork widened at its mouth, and, in what felt like a sigh, breathed us out into the wide channel of the Main Salmon. There was a stripe in the water where the two rivers met: the darker green water of the Main swallowing the bright indigo of the Middle Fork, obscuring all trace of it. Sheer granite walls receded behind us as the two rivers, now one, turned west, and we left the wilderness behind.

The grand finale was Cramer, a rowdy wave train with a humongous, raft-sucking hydraulic on river right. "We'll see the hole to the left, and we won't go into it," Frank assured us. "It's not complicated."

For the first time all week, he seemed almost giddy. To run the rapid, or be done with the trip and with me, I couldn't tell. But it didn't matter. I was happy to give him this moment, in gratitude for all he'd given me: safe passage through the most beautiful, wildest country I'd ever seen, so much of which I couldn't see, all the way, clearly, but which had nonetheless penetrated me, I could feel it. The narrow strip of sapphire sky above clear green water, the smoky scent of burnt trees, the soft brown hills—they were inside me now for good.

We bounced through Cramer's three-foot waves, doused and whooping with anticipation and release—a week's worth of tension coiled in our jaws set free.

I turned around to check on Steve. He was through, too, tucking his oars under his knees to catch his breath. I could tell by the way he turned to look behind him that he felt it, too. The canyon had been brilliant, almost unbearably lovely. It had sheltered us even as it tested us. What came next might very well be harder, but he'd seen it—all of it. I just wished we could have seen it together.

The river had been pushy and constricted, tougher and more technical than any whitewater I'd ever run, but it was not unfriendly. It was simply itself, coursing through the wilderness, dropping 2,000 feet in one hundred miles. It had been up to us to match its pace.

Part Two

CANYONS

11. BACK TO ZERO

Sometimes when I go outside to take a hot tub before bed, and Steve is already soaking, his bare skin bright in the blue moonlight, it hits me how long we have been together, how we have chosen each other to be with, forever, only, and for a second I think I might fall over, staggered by the magnitude of our choice, the one we made so long ago, when we were so far away from this moment and knew so little. And I wonder, briefly, who would we each be if we hadn't?

Once, years before Idaho, just after we married, Steve and I were on a plane flying west when we overheard a passenger in the row behind us announce excitedly, "Look, there's the Grand Canyon!" And as his seatmate leaned over to the window to admire the view, the man went on, his voice overcome by awe, "And the wildest thing is, there's a *river* down there!"

This is one of our all-time favorite lines, as though it were possible to have a canyon without a river having once carved through it, as though water were somehow incidental to the canyon, not its cause.

If rivers are the lifeblood of the desert, then canyons are the womb, the keeper of water. When you are inside a canyon, you cannot see out, only ahead, around the nearest bend. Canyons are the inverse of mountains: they behave in opposite ways. Entering a canyon, you must go down before you come up. It is warmer at the bottom of a canyon than at the top. To experience canyons is to be willing to open your mind and flip it upside down. Without flow there would be no canyons; canyons, too, create flow, channeling water between constricted walls. They invite the suspension of doubt and disbelief. Even when you can't see where you're going, a canyon will carry you there.

—

I thought that when we got to the end of the Middle Fork, the worst part would be over. I imagined Steve and me getting into the truck and pulling away, the magnitude of relief hitting with full force. We would stick our hands out the open window and wave as we left in a cloud of dust, bound for home.

I pictured the girls and dogs rushing out to welcome us, my mother standing behind them with a look of quiet determination on her face, ready to take care of us.

What I didn't envision was the two of us, cooped up in the truck for sixteen hours, barely saying a word. I lay splayed out in the backseat, the seatbelt contorted awkwardly around my waist and my leg raised on dry bags. I was wearing the same baggy turquoise river shorts I'd worn all week. My bathing suit was still damp. On the river, our mutual silence had felt necessary, capacious even, matched by the scale of the wilderness, but now in the cab of the truck it compressed around us, sharp and suddenly dangerous. I slumped on the driver's side, relieved not to be able to see Steve's face in the rearview mirror. There was too much to say, and I didn't know how to start.

We'd come out of the canyon, but we were still in it.

Now we come to the part of the story I've never told.

We drove without stopping all the way through southern Idaho, crossing the state line into Utah, making time on Salt Lake City's smog-choked freeways, past Provo and strange, docile Mormon towns, their giant initials etched with rocks into hillsides. Outside, the green hills of summer drifted by and, though I tried not to, I appreciated them and the way the sun hovered over the mountains, over the Great Salt Lake, and lit up the Wasatch Range. I didn't want to love anything that day, even the mountains, because I was too angry, so I lay mutely in the backseat, biting my tongue.

Somewhere north of Price, in the winding, sunbaked hills and blank towns. Exploding outward from the claustrophobic silence was my rage and Steve's regret and his rage at my rage, and pain—both of ours—and sadness that things hadn't turned out the way we'd pictured, and shame. So much shame I felt as though it might choke me. And then we were yelling at each other from backseat to front, our words a torrent of recrimination and fury. *Your fault, no yours. I hate you. Why didn't you? Take one more oar stroke. Be brave. Fall out the right way.*

I screamed until I was hoarse, and I thought the windows might shatter from the force of my fury. Steve screamed right back, and it didn't matter what we were saying because what we were really saying was

> *Why don't you—*
> *Take care of me.*
> *Trust me.*

In the truck in desolate, sun-blasted Utah on one of the first days of summer, a summer now ruined and ruinous, our old misplaced hatred hummed between us, even after we both fell quiet again and I dozed off while Steve steered us south toward New Mexico and still later when we climbed out at a gas station on Navajo land, downtrodden and weary from it all, the river and life and trying to be things to each other that we couldn't even be to ourselves.

I limped into the gas station using a bent metal tent pole that Frank had found for me beside the river. It was perfectly mangled into the shape of a cane, but on slippery tile floor, it sent me skidding. Wordlessly, Steve bent down, pulled my arms around his neck, and carried me on his back through the candy aisles. I caught sight of our reflection in the window—I was grubby, and Steve's beard had grown in after six days in the wilderness; we looked like meth addicts staggering among the jumbo-sized Junior Mints and Milk Duds, too oily and strung out to bother cleaning up. This did not embarrass me as much as fascinate me.

Who were we, and how did we appear to others, with our tanned sandal feet and peeling dirty skin? Secretly, I wanted to laugh, but that would signal that I wasn't mad any longer, and I was. Even then, I knew that, years later, it would be Steve piggybacking me around the Philips 66 south of Cortez and my bent tentpole cane clacking the floor on a parched late June day that I would remember most from the whole trip, maybe even forever.

An hour from Santa Fe, Steve turned onto an unpaved forest road and pulled over. I opened the door and lowered myself to balance on the edge of the foot rail, tugged down my shorts, and peed in the dirt. It was a relief, finally, to not care, to not see ourselves as others might see us, but to simply stop trying and to do what we needed to do, having no idea what might happen, and just keep going.

—

Home.

The concrete floor is cool in the night air. My mother has gotten our spare pair of crutches out of the gear shed. I crutch over the gleaming, smooth floor, marveling at how much easier it is to maneuver without bumps and rocks and lumps of grass. I can crutch all over the house on my own!

The thrill wears off instantly.

In the morning I call my doctor and explain what happened. "I need an MRI," I say. "Can you order one?"

"You need an X-Ray," Dr. G. replies. I like my doctor. He does not make a big deal of things that do not need to be made a big deal of. He knows better than to scare me with hypotheticals. Once, after my father died, I was so anxious in his office that Dr. G. played Tibetan sound bowls for me. "They'll help reset your nervous system," he explained. He'd gotten them in Nepal on a trekking expedition. He placed them next to my head as I lay on my back on the examining table and closed my eyes. The bowls rang, echoing outward through the room until they moved inside of me and I couldn't tell if they were ringing or I was, and I settled into a deep, calm wondering, at peace with a mystery that, for a moment, I did not need to solve.

I don't remember going in for an X-Ray, but I must have, because the next day, a Friday, Dr. G. calls.

"Well, Katie," he says with an audible sadness, "you fractured your tibial plateau. Badly. You're going to need surgery. I'm so sorry."

"Tibial *what*?"

"It's the bone in your leg where your tibia meets your knee," he explains. "The knobby bump on the outside." I feel for it on my right leg, the unbroken leg, and rub it, filled with a strange, sad wonder. I know I have a high pain tolerance, but that I rafted a river for six days with a broken leg is ridiculous, even for me.

He's scheduled me to see a trauma surgeon. I have to have surgery right away. "And Katie," he adds before hanging up, "the recovery is long. Fourteen weeks non-weight-bearing."

I sit on the kitchen stool and feel my bare feet on the smooth concrete. My crutches lean against the counter. Fourteen weeks. I do the math. The whole summer, the sweetest most golden season of lightness and luck and mountains and running. Every last day of it.

The surgeon. I go alone. Steve, busy with a backlog of client meetings, says, "I'll try to meet you there if I get free," but I can tell by his clipped tone that he probably won't, that he's just placating me, not because he doesn't want to come, but because he doesn't understand why I need him to.

The surgeon is slim, dark haired, about my age, and doesn't smile, except sardonically. All business. His smile is pressed flat, almost a smirk. My stepbrother smiles like this, only his smile is funny and punkish and says, *You're cool, I love you, you weird kid.* The doctor is not trying to hide his disdain. He's bored of broken bones.

The X-rays are bad, show a lot of damage. He will need to pin the bone back together. He sounds almost put out. "You stayed on the river?" The way he asks this, it doesn't sound brave, only stupid. He disappears for a time to talk to his assistant. I sit in the exam room alone and wrap my arms around myself. The air conditioning is too cold. I call Steve but he doesn't pick up.

When the surgeon comes back, I try to explain. "I run, I'm a runner. I write about this. It's what I do." But I must do a poor job expressing myself because he just stares at me flatly, and I try not to cry but fail and feel stupider for letting him see my tears.

The surgeon speaks in complete sentences, but my brain has fallen behind, and I only hear words. Fourteen weeks. Plate and screws. Long recovery. Pain.

I'm a runner. I'm used to pain. Doesn't this count for something? "My knee's been healing," I say hopefully. "I can feel it. I have less pain now than I did a week ago."

The surgeon laughs ruefully, with what sounds almost like pleasure. "Pain? Oh, don't worry, you're going to have pain again. I have to re-break it to fix it. I'm going to take you back to zero."

And there's one other thing. Even after his expert craftsmanship has healed completely, and the pain is finally gone, he says, "You'll have a high chance of developing arthritis in your knee."

Now I'm blubbering like a baby, and I don't even try to hide it. His mouth is a mean line. He shakes his head impatiently, like he sees these theatrics a hundred times a day and finds them tedious and irritating.

"Look, I used to play soccer, but after I blew out my knee, I had to stop. You should find a new hobby. Running is a terrible idea. If I were you, I'd never run again."

—

I take out my hatred for the surgeon on Steve, but my rage for the two men is so indecipherable and voluminous it's impossible to tell who I'm madder at. Probably me. I cried like a baby and let the surgeon patronize me. I hadn't stood up for myself, and now he's going to cut me open and put his cold instruments and his bad attitude into my body.

My friends try to reassure me. "He's a surgeon, not a therapist."

"His job is to repair the fracture. That's what you want from him. He doesn't have to be your friend."

They say, "Injury means you are living an adventurous life. It was bound to happen sometime."

And, "He's the best in town."

The fact is, I don't have time for a second opinion. It's been ten days since the accident, and my knee has to be mended before it heals in the wrong way.

I wake before first light the next morning, a flutter of excitement in my chest, the way I used to when I was running up the mountain every day. It was only ten days ago, but it already feels like forever. I know what I have to do. I figured it out in my sleep. I call the surgeon. His assistant picks up. "I'll have him call you back," she tells me. Less than five minutes later, my phone rings. It's him.

I can't believe he called me back, this soon or at all, so I haven't planned what I am going to say, but the words come strong and clear and unafraid from the deepest part of me. "I know you're going to do the best job you can, but before you do, I need to tell you that running is not a hobby for me. It's what I do as a writer and an athlete. It's my job and central to my life. I've always been a runner. I want you to know this."

The surgeon listens quietly. I can tell from his low tone that he's not smirking when he says, "Nothing you said will change how I approach the surgery. I'm still going to do the best job possible. But thank you for telling me this."

If he's going to heal me, he needed to hear me.

I wake after the operation in a blinding haze of fluorescent lights and confusion, talking about Washington, DC, where I was born. I must be talking because I hear my own voice, but I don't know where the words are coming from, or why. The person I'm telling is a nurse, who vaporizes and becomes Steve, bending over me, taking my hand.

"She's awake," the nurse voice says, and I reach for Steve, and he's there and then gone, and the ceiling is low and close, like a tunnel, and someone is patting my hand, asking about the pain, saying, "You need to rest, this will help you rest." The next time I wake up I'm in a proper room with walls, not curtains, and hours have passed, and I am still alive.

"Surgery went well," the orthopedist tells me, or maybe he tells Steve because I'm so out of it, and I have the distinct feeling—possibly opioid-induced paranoia—that the surgeon doesn't want to see me again, is afraid of me and my white-hot defiance. Just as I am secretly afraid of him. But it's okay because I am swimming on dry land, the ground moving beneath me, and even though a freight train is running back and forth over my leg, I am back to zero, and everything new starts now.

12. BROKEN

Injury is a skip in time, a record needle slipping its groove. When you can no longer move at your usual pace, life downshifts to a dream-like tempo. Time slows and widens; at the same time, it presents itself with a curious granularity, urgency: here I am, don't waste me.

Zen is famous for its fluid understanding of time. The time is always now, just as now always, inevitably, becomes the next moment. But time does not move only in one direction, forward. It goes in all directions all at once. It flows with our mind and memory, with our thoughts and words and energy. "Time constantly goes from past to present and from present to future . . . and from present to past," Suzuki Roshi muses in *Zen Mind*. Now-time is all time, all at once.

This is one of the trickier concepts in Zen. Injury makes it more visceral, but only just barely. The scale of time is still too baffling to dissect. Dogen famously wrote that a single day contains six billion moments. When I try to wrap my mind around this number, I picture a time-lapse video at warp speed, moments too numerous to count bleeding into each other like meteors streaking through a black sky. Every now and then, though, one moment pulses long enough for us to catch it briefly in our hands and step inside, and we discover that what appeared like a blink is as big as the universe, stretching forward and backward forever.

The summer Pippa was one, Steve and I took her rafting on the Rio Grande. It was August, and the sky was piercing, high-altitude blue shot through with clarity. The river ran low and calm with only a few riffles. We drifted idly downstream, stopping every so often to splash in the shallows.

That morning, I'd sat at the table in the shade of the covered porch—*portal*—and fed Pippa forkfuls of maple syrup–soaked pancake. She chirped happily between bites. Through the open kitchen door, I could hear a song playing on the radio. The lyrics wafting into the morning air seemed to hang there, suspended in time. *I'm thinking about eternity, some kind of ecstasy's got a hold on me.*

I can still see us sitting on the grassy riverbank, so much younger, in our bathing suits, eating peanut butter sandwiches beneath wide-brimmed straw hats, Pippa plump and soft in my arms. The feeling that arose in me was one of almost overwhelming contentment. I was exactly in the moment as it unfolded around me and folded me in, knowing with a strange clairvoyance that it was one of those days I would remember always for not being afraid, for not wanting time to slow down or speed up, for allowing it to move with its own energy and to carry us with it.

Afterward, we spent the night at an organic farm in Taos. We gathered eggs and Pippa scratched a burro behind its bristly ears. The owner served us homemade goat cheese, and we ate dinner at the picnic table late into the evening. It was high summer, and to the east a potbelly moon hung on the horizon like a counterweight to the sun, holding down the corners of the sky. Invisible though it was, I could feel it: this was the moment time shifted from the decadent slow crawl of baby-time to the speedier tick of real-time gathering itself, deciding to move. That day we stood on the cusp and the world tilted and tipped us forward, quickening, and we were off, into the rest of our lives.

I didn't know that soon I would be pregnant again, that my father would die, that life would accelerate, spinning ever faster. I didn't know that time is a circle without start or finish, infinite and impermanent. That you can pick it up anywhere and read it forward or back, like a book.

—

Now the days billowed open again, gauzy as cotton. No matter where I was, it was always now. All I did in those first weeks after surgery was sit around. In the car, on the couch, on porches, on chairs, in bed, on a chaise on the back patio. I got up each morning to sit back down. The irony of it would have been funny if it weren't so maddening.

My favorite place to sit was outside, at a small round table under the portal. My mother gave me the table when I bought my house in 2000. I'd lived in Santa Fe for five years by then, but I still wasn't sure if I was coming or going. I was in a holding pattern—vacillating between here and there, old life and new, what others thought was best for me and what I wanted for myself. I was raised to be a good girl who listened to her parents, pleased others, and followed standard procedure. Standard procedure was to stay on the East Coast, find a husband, have a career and kids, be ambitious but predictable. The problem was, being the good girl seemed like a bad idea.

"Well, I guess you're never going to marry an investment banker," my stepfather, Ron, himself an investment banker, said with a sigh a few weeks before I left New York for Santa Fe. It was 1995. I was twenty-three and quitting my full-time job as a book publicist to take a temporary position at a magazine that paid interns five dollars an hour to work sixty-hour weeks. Ron shook his head gloomily, as though he could see all my future disappointments unfurling before him, a series of missteps spiraling out from this one grievous error.

I bit my cheek, trying not to laugh. I couldn't recall a single instance when I'd aspired to his scenario.

Even after I settled in Santa Fe, though, I could still redeem myself by going back. That's what people did. They left to seek their way in the world, but then they went home. It wasn't too late for me. I was twenty-seven, unattached, my life still portable. I lived month-to-month in a 500-square foot guest house with a futon for a couch. Sometimes I thought I wanted to leave, especially on Saturday afternoons after I'd ridden my mountain bike with my friends for hours and come home, hot and hungry, and lugged my laundry basket on my hip down the dirt lane to the little laundromat on Palace Avenue. I'd sit on a plastic chair watching my bike shorts and T-shirts spin around and around, feeling alone and adrift with a skim of dried sweat on my skin, and wonder what it was that I thought I might be doing, all the way out on the edge of the desert, so far from my family.

One day, on a whim, I answered a classified ad for a house for sale. "Charming pitched-roof farmhouse blocks from the Plaza. Country setting in the middle of town!" it read in six-point print. I followed a labyrinth of dirt roads, few of them signed, all the addresses out of numerical order. The house I was looking for announced itself immediately as a strange and lovely anomaly: the stucco, unlike every other house in Santa Fe, wasn't lunch-bag brown but a vivid shade of undercooked salmon, the steeply pitched roof made from corrugated metal.

The owner, Joan, hugged me at the door and explained breathlessly that just yesterday she had buried a statue of St. Joseph, the patron saint of real estate, in the front garden! Joan was an eccentric artist-turned-puppeteer in her mid-fifties with frizzy blonde hair who fancied herself a bit of a seer. When she built the house a decade earlier, she'd tucked plastic film canisters filled with recipes, positive affirmations, and love notes into the wall beams. She'd buried at least two, possibly three, pet Scotty dogs in the backyard. Though she didn't give me details, I understood that she had been lonely in the pink house, but now she'd found true love and a second husband and was moving her puppet sets and paintbrushes to his place across town.

Inside, the white plank ceilings were sixteen feet tall and braced with beams shaped like the ribs of an overturned boat. The rooms were airy and bright, with old windows salvaged from the South, and I wanted it immediately, this strange ship house run aground in the desert. I had just enough for a down payment, and my salary at the magazine would cover the monthly mortgage.

I knew it was mine, and not because Joan told me "the energy is right." I felt it myself, fast and clear, deep in my bones, all the way to my feet. Sometimes decisions take forever, and sometimes they happen in an instant.

A few weeks before I moved in, Joan invited three of my closest friends and me over for dinner-slash-housewarming seance-slash-ceremonial transfer of power. Candles were lit and intentions murmured, Joan simultaneously conjuring up her former heartbroken self and my future jubilant self, as though by inhabiting her house I would inherit her good fortune and her happy ending would become mine.

As we bowed our heads gravely, Joan turned to me and pronounced, "Now that you're committing to this place, you will meet a man. The universe senses these things, you know." I caught my friend Elizabeth's eye and suppressed a nervous giggle.

Three months after I signed the papers, I met Steve. I was walking my new puppy, and he was walking off a field after playing Ultimate Frisbee with the husband of one of my friends. Tan legs, calico hair. He strode straight toward me, as if he knew me, looking at me as if into me.

This is the part of the story I always tell: he smiled at me with his one deep dimple. Then he got down onto the grass and slow-motion wrestled my puppy, like we were in a rom-com.

There he is, I thought. That's the guy.

It would be five more years before we got married, but every night in the summers that followed, Steve and I sat at the small stone table under the portal, eating tomatoes for dinner, listening to the crickets, feeling complicit in something: a simple, good life, outside, together.

It was here at this table, I decided, that I would put my convalescence to good use. Now that I couldn't go up the mountain, now that I was forced to sit, I had all the time in the world. My book deadline loomed, and I could finally get serious about meditation.

I actually thought this. Believed it. Wrote it in my notebook in a flood of determined, caffeine-fueled optimism-slash-delusion.

I will sit at this table and get ...

Here the entry trails off without explanation, as if I suddenly realized my forced enthusiasm was a sham even I couldn't write my way into.

—

This was where Natalie found me when she came to visit—installed at my table, a permanent exhibit: *Writer at Work? Still Life with Crutches*. The air felt healing, and I had a clear view of the driveway from my seat, so I could see friends when they arrived with dark chocolate bars, soup for lunch, protein smoothies, books on Buddhism, poetry collections. I jokingly referred to these visits with friends as my "porch salon," but I knew that it was their kindness that would save me, far more than my writing, which was atrophying as fast as my leg.

Natalie settled onto the iron-backed chair next to me and frowned. "How do you sit here all day?" she asked incredulously. "This chair is so uncomfortable." I looked down, as though appraising it for the first time. The seat pad was thin, starting to fray around the seams, and the slats, hard and unforgiving, jabbed into my spine.

"You look so twisted," Natalie went on, sounding displeased. "If you're relaxed in your body, your writing is relaxed, and this is better writing." It was true for running, too. When I'm tight and fraught, I might run fast for a while, but I won't flow.

I told her I was blocked. Now that I couldn't move my body, I was having trouble moving my mind.

"Writing doesn't care if you have a broken leg," she said flatly. This is one of the best things about Nat: she never lies to make you feel better, which almost always makes me feel better.

She held one palm up in front of my face. "You know what this means?" she asked. "You're at the edge. You're up against the wall."

I sighed. "I'm broken, you're rising." I could say these things to her; Natalie and I didn't compete with each other. She'd recently gone through cancer and was in remission, and feeling sorry for myself didn't change how relieved I was for her, nor did being glad for her make me less depressed about my leg.

"It's the same thing, don't you see?" Natalie went on. "I wouldn't be alive and awake and burning hot if I hadn't once been up against the wall."

She stood up abruptly. "I'm going home to get you a better chair, this one's ridiculous. You'll see. I think we're going to have fun this summer."

—

The next time Natalie comes over, she's carrying a plastic Adirondack lounge chair with a thick brown cushion in one hand and a plastic bag of marijuana in the other.

The new chair has a reclining back that makes me feel like I should be watching TV in a hospital bed; the pot is medical marijuana left over from her cancer treatment. From a canvas tote bag, she extracts a small, neat box that looks like it might hold cigars or a fine necklace and opens it as though presenting me with her family jewels. Inside is a gleaming, red metal tin the size of a cellphone and bright as lipstick. It resembles a very large cigarette lighter or a gun case, glossy and slightly sinister. I have no idea what it is.

"It's a vaporizer, Katie," she says, grinning at my naiveté.

"So I don't have to…?" I trail off and purse my lips in a noisy, exaggerated inhale.

"Smoke it?" she asks, laughing at my imitation. "No. You just breathe in. It's much easier on your lungs."

I cast a furtive glance into the house. The babysitter is dusting the bookshelves. Pippa and Maisy are at day camp, but we are paying the sitter extra to clean because the house is a disaster of dirty dishes and dust bunnies. This is one benefit of injury: you get used to pink Bermuda shorts left in a ball in the middle of the hallway, everywhere a trail of clothes and toys and miscellany, bread crumbs in the daily mystery of young girls' lives. You have to crutch by. You have to let go.

I make a mental list of all the reasons I can't get high: I'm an ultra runner, I need my lungs; the babysitter is plumping pillows in the next room; I don't *do* drugs. Even when I was in high school and everyone I knew was smoking pot, I steered clear. I wanted to experience the real thing, not an enhancement or exaggeration, not a wobbly hallucination, but the moment as it was. I guess I was a little bit Zen even then.

As though reading my mind, Natalie holds up her hand and says, "I think it could really help with the pain. Try."

The surgical nurse had sent me home with sixty opioid pills, doctor's orders. Sixty! Just the thought of them in my medicine cabinet freaked me out. Far better to vape a little pot than get hooked on painkillers, become an addict, and die in a gutter somewhere.

"Okay," I tell Natalie.

She raises the lipstick-looking vaporizer to her mouth, pushes a button, and takes a long, dramatic drag. The pungent scent of marijuana fills the air. Her mouth slides into a wide, slow smile. She hands the case to me and I fumble it into position, inhale furtively, and hold my breath, vapor scraping my throat.

I feel the tickle of one tiny giggle rising inside me and try to look stern. "Nat, you know we're not going to sit here getting stoned and eating potato chips all summer," I inform her, choking back guilty laughter.

"Absolutely not," she answers, her lips smashed together in a thin, hysterical line. But already my hilarity has subsided like a sneeze snuffed out. My leg is still broken, and now I feel nothing.

The sun is falling down behind the piñon trees, casting the porch in deep shadow, when Natalie stands to go, waving her stash at me. "I'm leaving this here with you." I think of what she'd said the last time she came over: artists need a quiet rock at their back. We are constantly putting our wild energy into the world, and without calmness, we will burn out. Her teacher, Katagiri Roshi, told her this. I knew she meant the steadiness of zazen, but I don't want to meditate, I want to move. I want to be wild, in my old ways.

I take the vaporizer out of its container, push the button, and watch the red light flick on. Then off. On. Yes, it could be that kind of summer. Or it could be the summer I sit and write like crazy, remembering everything before I forget.

"You better get busy," Natalie calls over her shoulder as she leaves. "Fourteen weeks isn't much time."

13. NO GOOD, NO BAD

My bicycle is mint green, with seven speeds, fenders, a bell, and a handlebar basket. It's attached to a metal stand on the back patio. Steve has removed the left pedal and in its place, he sets down a kitchen chair topped with a pile of pillows for height and padding. Carefully I climb onto the saddle, propping my brace on the pillow tower. This is the bike I ride around town on errands. Today I'm going to ride it one-legged in place in the backyard.

I push the pedal around and around with my right foot in a low gear, barely breaking a sweat. I think about how long I will have to sit on this foam seat biking with one leg in order to get my heart rate above one hundred. Steve, watching from the doorway on his way out to work, sees the discouragement on my face and says quietly, "Dig deep."

I set the timer on my phone for twenty minutes and shift into a higher gear, and before long, I'm sweating through my shirt. Within a few days I'm up to forty-five minutes. It's a far cry from running up the mountain, but I know I'm building more than my aerobic base. I'm banking hope.

Three times a week I drive myself to physical therapy. The therapist explains that our first goal is to regain range of motion. His name is Christopher, and he's ten years younger than I am and a competitive cyclist. He smiles too much at the parts of the story that aren't funny—falling out of the raft—and spends more time talking about his mountain bike racing than what I can do to heal my leg. Maybe I'm the problem, I wonder, closing my eyes while he helps me bend and straighten my leg in minuscule increments that seem almost promising.

But then Christopher smiles his rabid, overeager grin and says, "You know, running is so hard on your knees. I mean, it's brutal.

Mine just can't take it." I crack my eyes, and he's smiling a little, but not good-naturedly, more of a snicker.

I cock my head. Did he really just say that? He must have, because he's grinning broadly now, with a kind of triumph, the triumph of his good sense to ride his bicycle instead of run, and it's so convincing, his assurance, that I think about saying nothing, just lying there while he puts his pessimism into my broken leg. But then I remember what the surgeon said, and I sit partway up on my elbow and say, "No."

My voice is loud in the quiet treatment room. Christopher pauses, his hand on my broken leg, still grinning. It's like an assault, his smile. "Don't you see?" I ask. "If you believe that negative story about running while you're trying to heal me so I can run again, the therapy won't work. Your mindset matters as much as mine. Healing is mental, too."

Christopher's face has gone blank. I keep going. "Believing that running is bad for my knees isn't going to help my knee get better. It's a contradiction, doing physical therapy on my leg and saying those things." I think back to all the years I've been a runner, running through the confusion of childhood, the disequilibrium of becoming a mother, and the grief of losing my father. "Running may hurt you, but it doesn't hurt me. It heals me."

Christopher ducks his chin and nods, looking chastened. "I get it," he says, but I can tell he's never considered this. I might as well be speaking a foreign language. My words surprised me, too, but now that they're out, I know they're true. I have to believe in complete healing. I have to surround myself with people who believe it, too. I have to see it and feel it and live it. I have to train my mind to heal my body.

—

It's the night before our tenth wedding anniversary. After dinner, Steve and the girls and I squish together on the couch, going through our wedding albums, studying every picture. We look so young! Impossibly lovely, not at all haggard, our unlined faces full of hope. There was so much joy that weekend—laughter and dancing and skinny-dipping in the lake—that for a split second after we close the last page, I forget and think I can get up and walk. My brain has tricked me into believing I am the younger woman in the photographs, able-bodied and strong.

It's the oddest sensation, this momentary confusion. It's my body healing. This is how it works: my mind transporting me back to a time when I was healthy, and, at the same time, ahead to when I will be again.

I dream about walking. The setting and characters change, but the plot is always the same: I'm injured and on crutches and then, without thinking, I take one free step and then another. It is too soon, but I'm doing it: I'm walking across the room or down the road. I have left my crutches in another room or forgotten them; sometimes there's a witness—an old friend or Tom Hanks wearing roper boots or Steve—and I'm shocked that I am walking and afraid that I might be jeopardizing my recovery, and sometimes I am secretly thrilled. But I am always, always surprised.

This isn't denial. It's the opposite: it's my mind saying *patience*. My imagination doing its work, healing myself while I sleep. The most important thing is to get very strong, not just on the bike, but in everything I do—in what I see in my mind and in all my interactions and conversations, especially with myself.

Now when people ask me about the accident, I gloss over details and tell them instead about how I'm recovering. I no longer refer to my left leg as my broken leg: it's my healing leg. I am careful when I write in my notebooks to use the present tense. Recovery isn't something that will happen. It *is* happening.

> *My body is healing quickly and naturally and completely.*
> *It is healing.*

Even these words can be refined. Healing isn't a mysterious, passive process that's happening to me, but one that I am creating.

> *I am healing myself.*
> *Yes.*

I know better than to assume meditating will be easier with a broken leg. Sitting still is still hard. Maybe even harder.

Sometimes I'm relaxed and resigned, other times as restless as when I was ten, forced to sit through church sermons in itchy tights. I close my eyes and count my breaths to ten and then start over again. Five minutes, ten tops. Even when I'm restless and my leg throbs in its metal brace, it's peaceful to sit in the garden before the sun climbs high in the sky. Our dog Pete lies beside me, panting softly.

I have many thoughts, hundreds of them, between when I start at one and get to ten, but I've learned that the purpose of meditation is not to have no thoughts but rather to practice not following those thoughts—to note them, let them pass, and come back to your breath. One, *I'm angry at Steve*. Two, *I wish he'd taken another oar stroke off the rock*. Three, *what will I make for breakfast?*

I make concessions. I decide that it's okay to feel restless when I sit. It's okay to be angry and irritated and also afraid. It's totally normal to want to quit. It's not cheating to peek at the silken hummingbird beating the air with wings so delicate it appears to hover, motionless, in mid-air.

I notice the sky the way I notice the hummingbirds: with a shy, furtive wonder. It is a dusty, cornflower blue. Diaphanous clouds float like fingerprints over the mountains. It's mid-July, and even at 9:00 a.m., it's a sky blazingly weary of the sun; below, the land is an enormous, wavering mirage puckering beneath its own heat. It's okay to think about the rain, to wonder when the monsoon rains will come and how we will live as humans on this warming planet, our daughters especially, and if my writing will ever flow again.

> *Sat this morning on my meditation cushion on the patio outside bedroom. Wasn't all that comfortable. Sat in an ant pile by accident. They crawled up into my leg brace but I swatted them off and kept sitting. My mind was as scattered as my body and the ants crawling around but it was okay.*

It's tempting to judge the way we sit or how we meditate. Today was good, we say, I did it well. Or yesterday was hard. But really, there's no such thing as being "good" at meditation. Zazen isn't a performance or a competition; you can't compare yourself to others, or even to yourself. There are no measurable results and thus no pressure to do anything special. Simply showing up is the point. Doing it.

With every passing week, I'm becoming friendlier with myself, meeting my mind with small kindnesses. I see that I don't have to banish thoughts or make them cheerful. I just have to acknowledge them, note the fuss inside my head the same way I met the mountain when I ran up it, some days with a thrilling effortlessness, other days with unwanted difficulty. Running has taught me how to accept both. I used to run up a mountain; now I can sit like one.

When I try to explain this to Natalie, she nods and says, "No good, no bad." I've heard her use this phrase before. It's one of the central ideas in Zen that when we move beyond seeing life in black and white, in dualities, we release our fixed ideas of ourselves and the world and instead see the richness and possibility in each moment. No good, no bad—just this.

It was like the children's book I used to read aloud to Pippa and Maisy at bedtime when they were very small: a giant panda named Stillwater is told a Zen story of a man who breaks his leg. "Bad luck," his neighbors tell the man after each successive difficulty that befalls him. Each time, the man simply remarks, "Maybe." In the end, after a chain of unanticipated events, we learn that the man's broken leg saved him from going to war. All unknown consequences will reveal themselves in time, the story teaches us. What seems like misfortune may in fact be a lucky break.

I had trouble getting on board with this idea at first. It seemed bogus, frankly. Of course there is good and bad in the world; terrible things happen to people, catastrophic things, atrocities, and there isn't always a silver lining. That my broken leg might be a form of liberation seems wildly paradoxical, in its own way mind-twistingly awesome. I want it to be true, but it is still too soon to tell.

One day in the backyard, though, I am getting up when I feel like falling down. Something has come over me. I know it without naming it. It's joy. How is this possible in such a summer? But it is. It doesn't come from the sky or the hummingbirds or sitting by the fountain, or from the dog breathing rhythmically or something good about to happen or having just happened. No, the joy comes from nothing, and everything, from the moment itself: happiness and sorrow intertwined, in equal measure, in the exact same instant.

—

A few evenings later, I go with Steve to his Ultimate Frisbee game in a park near our house. The girls are away with my family, and I sit on the sidelines with his friends and teammates and try to remember the last time I watched Steve play. It takes him ten steps to run the length of the field. He's still so fast and lean, and it's easy to be the spectator—it requires nothing extra of me to cheer his name when he stretches out his long arm and catches a pass in midair in the end zone.

The sun is setting by the time we get in the car to go home. I've barely been away from the house in weeks, and the evening light is caramel, sweet and rich, the kind that makes you wish July would never end.

"Let's not go home just yet," I say, and Steve smiles out of the corner of his mouth and keeps driving, past the turnoff to our house to a dirt road I've never been on before that climbs steeply into the foothills. I crane my head this way and that. Looking is almost like traveling. You get ideas when you look. All the car windows are open, and the air coming down from the mountains smells damp and sweet, like it's finally going to rain.

14. RUNNING ON THE PAGE

When I ride the bike one-legged in the backyard, I listen to ultra running podcasts. This is not a form of torture but of transference. My leg gets sweaty and hot in its thick brace, but I barely notice because I'm enthralled by accounts of people running through the night on mountainous trails, eating cake frosting from a can, running through exhaustion clear out the other side into elation. I know this feeling, not just because I've felt it before, but because, for the first time since I fell out of the raft, I'm certain I will feel it again.

Natalie has given up on getting me high. Now when she comes over, we do writing practice together. I'm on the portal with her, but in my imagination I'm in Colorado, running one hundred miles. It's a clear morning and we start before dawn. I've been training for half a year but also my whole life for this run. I know I'm prepared as I toe the line because my legs tell me so, and my knees are strong, and I'm not in any hurry. I have all day. I am climbing to the tops of 14,000-foot mountains, and wildflowers are bright pink and purple, and there are snowy couloirs above me. I can feel the alpine sun on my bare arms, my friends are waiting for me at aid stations with miso soup and hot green tea. A zillion glittery stars hang overhead in the night. When I lick my wrist, I taste salt. And though I'm sitting at my table on a July afternoon in 2016 and my leg is in a brace healing from a fall, I am running in my mind, and my feet aren't touching the ground.

I make a deal with myself. I can write anything I want as long as I write something.

I write about the rock. How much I hate the rock. The pointy jagged rock dividing the river, and us, in two. We tried to go left but it sucked us right.

Steve crying, "Oh *fuck!*"

Riding a chute of water over the cobbled river bottom, banging everything, changing everything.

Life, like the boat, going upside down in an instant. We are no longer attached; we are forcibly detached.

I fill five pages about the rock and when I finish, I'm flushed and tired, but also energized, like I just drank three cups of coffee.

Like I just . . . *ran*.

I'm sitting in Natalie's lounger, with my foot propped up on the chair next to me. My toes are still slightly swollen, coddled, no longer doing the hard work of running or writing.

That's when I realize I write with my legs and my feet as much as my hands. I can get the same rush from writing as I do from running. I can run on the page.

—

After we buried my uncle Phil's ashes in upstate New York, I went back to my sad little motel overlooking a long lake. I sat in the weedy grass and looked out at the water. Far off in the middle, a sailboat with a white sail beat back and forth across the wind. It followed the same two tacks on the wave-scalloped water, slicing the lake with its bow, gaining no ground. I wondered what it must feel like to travel for no reason, to cross time and space without deviation, making little apparent progress and not needing to.

I think about that sailboat now, how peaceful it looked, how utterly ordinary and marvelous and free it must be to move doggedly and yet patiently, with tremendous stamina but no hurry or ambition.

Maybe if I can tap into the energy of running without running and bring it into my writing, I'll be able to finish my book about my father and trick my body into believing I'm healthy and whole again—like looking at those pictures in our wedding album, like the sailboat gaining ground because it's not trying to gain ground.

—

Injury fills me with a curious emptiness. It's like nothing I've felt before. It's not tranquility or contentment, nor equanimity or peace. I try to name it, but it's too slippery for description. If I were to name it, it would become something, when what it is, is an absence. I am scooped out, raw, open. Hollow. A house torn down to its studs, the hinges exposed, rattling in the wind.

It's not exactly unpleasant, just unfamiliar.

At its best, running is a true expression of the deepest part of me, but at its worst, it's a crutch that feeds my ego; how attached I've grown to the word *runner*. A noun, not a verb. Implying stasis, permanence, solidity. A label I've dressed myself up in for years, beneath which gapes a great, billowing, empty unknown. My uncertainty seems fundamental, overdue—destabilizing, yet somehow also constructive. Who am I now?

Who *am* I?

This is one of the most famous Zen koans, a simple inquiry to be asked over and over for a lifetime. Who am I? Sit with the question, in all the seasons, beside the river, on a mountain, in your backyard, deep in a canyon at dawn. *Who* am I? Ask it enough times and it will be like seeing the spelling of a familiar word you know by heart but suddenly no longer recognize. The answer keeps changing. Also, it will never change.

Maybe this is what the surgeon meant by going back to zero: discovering that we aren't who we think we are. We are so much more.

15. RANGE

My dreams have changed. Now, instead of walking, I'm running. In one dream I'm at the Empire State Building. The sign in the lobby says admission is five dollars for runners and ten dollars to ride the elevator. I pay five dollars. Then the dream sequence cuts to the observation deck, where I'm sweaty and tired from running all the way to the top. Another night, I'm in London, only it looks like California in springtime, wild and green and hilly, with long views to the bays, and Steve and I go out on the trails, and soon enough I am running; I run for an hour or more, feeling no pain, but then I remember it has not been ten weeks, and *I am supposed to still be on crutches*.

I'm not there yet, but almost.

One morning I wake up woozy, as though a part of me is missing, left behind in a dream. My brace is on my leg, my body is in the bed, my daughters are rattling dishes in the kitchen. So, what is it? The answer comes through my body, through the soles of my feet. It's not motion, but range that is missing—traveling across distance and space, leaving home and coming home. It's the away-ness and wildness I miss most, maybe even more than running.

I count the weeks from surgery. Each one brings me closer to walking. It's like counting the rapids in the river all over again; some day in the not-so-distant future, it will be like counting the days of quarantine. Focus on the rapid, the day, the breath, right in front of you. You can get through almost anything this way.

Beneath my brace, dried, dead skin on my shin is peeling and flaking off. I'm a snake shedding its skin, sloughing off old parts, being reborn. My body is becoming softer and smaller, my legs shrinking. I am being unformed to be re-formed.

I'm sitting all the time but no longer fighting it. I am dreaming of running, mountains and running. Even rivers.

One weekend in late August, we pack our camping gear and drive north, looking for water. Steve knows a good place. Just over the border in Colorado, we turn west onto a dirt road leading into the Rio de Los Pinos watershed. The grass is green from monsoon rains, and tuxedo-breasted magpies flock the valley. Soon cow pastures and crumbling adobes give way to a rugged, narrow canyon. The Los Pinos runs swift and clear, little more than eight feet across and barely knee-deep. No one will die or break a leg on this river, I'm sure of it. It's perfect.

We set up camp in a small meadow on the bank. After dinner, while Steve and the girls kick a soccer ball in the long grass, I crutch upstream along the dirt road. It's nearly dusk and the river's already in shadow, but the tips of the fir trees glow tangerine in the sunset. The river gurgles its low, soft song beside me. My mood matches the water's: quiet, buzzing with a low, persistent hum, a feeling I've known all my life. I am part of the world, and it is part of me.

The river purrs all night while we sleep. In the morning, while Steve casts for trout, the girls and I sit with our notebooks propped open in our laps and do writing practice. "Write about apples, anything you want about apples," I suggest. "Ten minutes, go."

When the time's up, I ask Maisy if she wants to read aloud what she wrote. She shakes her head no. "Mama, it's mostly just about the wild," she says. "I am a wild girl in nature, and my mama is, too."

In early September, the orthopedist gives me the green light to bear weight. I'm only allowed to bear thirty pounds on my left leg, with the aid of crutches, for the next four weeks, but I can walk! When I put my foot down, it feels odd and tingly, electric charges surging up and down through the ball of my foot, nerve endings re-acclimating to the earth. It's time to dig out all my left shoes and wear both again, like a normal person.

The surgeon no longer scares me the way he once did. His opinion of my progress and prospects is incidental, not essential. I've learned the power of my own resilience. I'm writing my own story, and it's different from his.

—

On the first day of fall, I fly to a writing residency in New Hampshire to finish my book about my father. I was accepted earlier in the summer but wasn't sure I'd be healed enough to go on my own. I carry my crutches with me on the plane, just in case, but as soon as I arrive, I stash them in the back of the closet in my room and forget all about them.

The residency has a fleet of ancient, three-speed steel loaner bikes for getting around campus. The one I choose is dark green and rusting, with a creaky chain and a wicker handlebar basket. It's so heavy I have to stand up on the pedals to make it up even the smallest hills. I love it immediately, unreservedly.

I go everywhere by bike: down steep dirt roads on rotten coaster brakes, to and from my studio in the woods, into town, out to a pond a few miles away. After months of immobility, biking is the pinnacle of freedom. Around campus, lights are on in the artists' cottages as I pass; poets and playwrights are hunched studiously over their desks. The Irish war photographer who brought his racing bicycle and rides one hundred miles in a day has dragged his desk outside, and I wave euphorically as I pass, as though drunk on adrenaline and joy. His bicycle is making him fast. Mine is making me whole.

When I ride, I feel like I'm seven again, flying along suburban New Jersey streets with my feet off the pedals and legs flung into the air—the age I was when I discovered what seemed like the true secret to human happiness: moving my body to make something in my mind.

I'm in New Hampshire for three weeks, while Steve holds down the fort in Santa Fe. As with most tasks, he appears unflappable in the face of solo parenting. I don't hear much from home: at most a phone call late in the evening while I'm still writing in my studio and it's bedtime in Santa Fe. This time, his silence feels generous, as though he's sparing me from the distractions of daily life so I can focus on my work.

With no one to look after but myself, my time is utterly my own. I can wake early and ride my bike or meditate for a few minutes in the garden before breakfast and then write straight through until lunch. I can do laps on my bike after dinner, writing in my head as I ride. I can stay up after midnight, reading. The freedom is outrageous, thrilling, like nothing I've known since having children. It feels almost showy to be so full of feral energy, as though I'm breaking an unspoken code of writerly conduct by having this much fun.

The more I ride, the faster the words pour out of me. I have to keep reminding myself that even though it doesn't feel like it, I'm working. My time here is legitimate: my work has value; my writing, meaning. This is surely one of the more depressing realities of being a woman: that we still feel we must justify our work in the world, our time away from home, as much to ourselves as to our partners, families, and society.

On the surface, Steve and I have an equal partnership, but I feel badly that he does most of the cooking and that my earnings are erratic, often far less than his. My shame is as old as my joy, and below that is a nameless fury that isn't mine alone but feels as though it belongs to all of womankind, to the ghosts of all the mothers who came before me. The shame and rage are so intricately entwined it's hard to peel them apart.

Steve and I never talked about it explicitly. We never said, "I'll quit my magazine job to pursue my dream of writing and will make a minuscule fraction of what I used to earn, and you will become the sole steady breadwinner and carry the burden of supporting us until you're simmering with silent resentment." Why hadn't we said those things? We both came from families where silence was the default mode of communication. Unwittingly, over time, we adopted it as ours. For our wedding, in 2006, we hired a woman to sing the musical interlude, Alison Kraus's "When You Say Nothing at All." We couldn't have predicted then the sacrifices the other would make, often willingly, in order to raise our daughters the way we'd imagined.

"Keep your oar in the water," my mother advised me shortly before Pippa was born. I loved her metaphor, it was so my mother! She meant don't give up your career as a writer, but keep at it, even just a little, to earn money and stay in the game. She hadn't had this option: after my father left when I was three and my sister five, she went back to school to get her CPA degree and later worked full-time to support us. For years afterward, my parents didn't talk about that either.

Nothing can prepare you for the cosmos-altering effects of parenting. Steve and I suddenly had a small human to care for, to keep alive. It was an all-consuming task—exhausting and exquisite, a prolonged act of pure animal instinct. I took my mother's advice to heart—I stopped traveling on assignment and instead pitched stories that I could report from my writing loft, while Pippa napped downstairs in her crib. What little time, energy, and brain cells I had left went into my writing.

Sometimes in the heat of my resentment, I thought of a line I'd read by Deborah Levy, in her memoir *Things I Don't Want to Know*: "Now that we were mothers we were shadows of our former selves, chased by the women we used to be before we had children. We didn't really know what to do with her, this fierce, independent young woman."

Only now *I* was chasing her: the person I was before I became a mother, who rode her bike up and down mountains, trying to race the darkness home. She was still in me somewhere, amidst the seemingly endless chaos and mess, the curve balls and contradictions, the towels on the floor and the Band-Aid wrappers stuck to the edge of the sink, the almost unbearable tenderness of everyday life. I missed her. I was a little in awe of her.

Now, wheeling around the woods in New Hampshire, I think about how to be a wife and a mother and the girl I used to be all at once, how to protect what I'd accidentally stumbled on as a child that felt secretive and powerful and a little bit dangerous. Was it selfish, knowing how to love and be alive in the world? Did anyone deserve to be so happy, riding their bike and running up hills and writing stories?

We all have habits that make our hearts sing, only we forget them. We get sidetracked and busy, focused on phones and deadlines and serious, grown-up responsibilities and children to feed and love and parents to care for and bills to pay, and we decide that joy is optional. Maybe even frivolous.

When, in fact, it's essential.

—

"Do you think you'll ever come back to the Middle Fork?" Frank asked me, near the end of our trip, when chances seemed good that we would get down the river safely.

I didn't have to think about it. "Yes," I said. I wanted to float the Middle Fork with Steve and our girls, on two healthy legs. I wanted to follow the trail along the bank and scramble up side canyons to waterfalls and see everything I'd missed.

Anything is possible, still ahead, as it always is. We just forget sometimes. A rupture is a fracture between old and new, a reminder that reinvention is possible every day. I could ride a bike across the country, write a novel, run one hundred miles.

I could go anywhere in my mind.

We all can.

—

My range has returned at last.

The final lines of my book fall out of me in a whoosh one morning in mid-October. Just in time—I'm flying home to Santa Fe the next day. I take one last spin on my bike through the woods, out to the pond where all the leaves in the trees have turned crimson and gold, as pretty as a jigsaw puzzle photograph.

It's uphill all the way back to my studio, and I pedal fast up the climb. My legs have gotten so much stronger. I can sense Steve and the girls rising up in me, pulling me in. It's time to go home, back to mothering and being a wife, writing in speed intervals at the edges of my days, in the middle of everything.

I can't wait to go, and I want to stay. I've finally made peace with the paradox. Resistance and acceptance live simultaneously, sometimes in the very same breath. Almost always in the same breath. No good, no bad. Each breath in and out—perfectly, imperfectly complete.

I look around, trying to memorize it my mind: the scarlet foliage and the rusty wet grass at the edge of the pond, the cloudless sky and the moon on its way to full, the war photographer at his desk and my clunky green bike and the wind in my ears, how it feels to move with so much energy, inside and out.

I'm searching for something. I don't know what, exactly, and I do. Glimmers of ideas, wonders, stories, joy. Always.

Part Three

MOUNTAINS

16. ZEN MIND, RUNNER'S MIND

The strange and beautiful thing about mountains is that the closer you are to them, the smaller they appear. From a distance mountains tower over you, but as you approach, they seem to shrink, almost disappear. They become the trees in front of you, rocks under your feet, bits and pieces of a bigger picture. Don't think about climbing the whole mountain, just start with what's in front of you, the ground beneath your feet. Do this, step by step, and eventually you'll reach the top.

I don't know I'm going to start running again until I do. It's New Year's Eve, which always makes me simultaneously melancholy and hopeful. I'm on Atalaya, cresting the summit and descending the steep north side. I left early, before the others were awake, and the trail is blanketed in a spongy padding of overnight snow. I've been hiking up Atalaya all fall, being patient, waiting, listening for my body to tell me it's time. The mountain is smaller once again, restored to its original proportions, and I still know all its sections by heart, as though I've never been away.

When I reach the craggy saddle, the trail flattens out, hugging the ridge line in a well-mannered way that still manages to feel a little wild. There's something about this little curl of trail that always sets my heart loose in my chest. Today it sounds like singing. It sounds like running.

And then I am.

My legs, operating independently from my mind, break into a spontaneous jog, more like skipping at first, a tentative shuffle. It feels slow but . . . normal; I shuffle along another ten strides. Springs and stuffing are not exploding outward from my knee! "Look at me, Pete, I'm running!" I cry to my dog, but he doesn't answer, of course, or even turn around. He trots ahead of me, black ears flapping, as though we've always run up the mountain together and will always run up the mountain together.

I jog carefully the rest of the way down. My knee feels stable, but my head is on fire with happiness. How I've missed this! And learned to be without it.

—

It was around this time that Natalie came over with the book. She was barely inside the front door when she pulled a paperback copy of *Zen Mind, Beginner's Mind* from her ratty cotton purse.

"Here," she said, waving it unceremoniously in front of my face. "I brought you this. It's time you read it."

Zen Mind, Beginner's Mind was slim, its pale gray cover adorned in wispy calligraphy. Even then, the book exuded an aura of age, of having been paged through again and again, though nothing about its appearance indicated it was anything but brand new.

Inside, she'd inscribed it in her large, loopy handwriting, "For Katie, my great honor of presenting you your lifetime Zen copy. All my love, Natalie."

To her students around the world, Natalie is an insightful Zen practitioner and teacher, but for as long as we've been friends, we've talked about Zen in a different way—by talking about life. All summer under the portal, we talked about how a broken leg might seem on the surface to be a bad thing, but could you really say that it was? Now that I was running again, I couldn't say that. It just . . . was. It had been the summer we waited for rain and I walked with my hands, balancing on my crutches for so long that callouses thickened my palms. It was the summer the girls got lice and I had to rake their hair with a metal comb twice a day. I missed that, touching them so intimately and deliberately. It was the summer I crawled onto the flat roof to watch the sun rise over mountains. It was the summer I ran in my mind.

I turned the book over in my hands. *Zen Mind, Beginner's Mind* is a collection of Dharma talks that Shunryu Suzuki gave at the San Francisco Zen Center in the late 1960s and seventies. The back cover features a full-page black-and-white photograph of the author. He is bald, with a penetrating gaze, two days of stubble, and the slightest suggestion of a smile. According to the bio, Suzuki Roshi died of stomach cancer in December, 1971, a month after I was born. I'd never heard of him or his book before.

I wasn't making a big deal of running. Maybe I hadn't even told Natalie I'd started again, though probably I had. Either way, the book didn't seem to have anything to do with running. It was about sitting. A *lot* of sitting. Natalie warned me that I might not get it, but I was between books. I might as well try.

Suzuki Roshi was talking about zazen, but as soon as I started reading, I realized that if I replaced "sitting" with running, he and I were speaking the same language. After all, the main principles of Zen—form, repetition, stamina, impermanence, suffering, awakening—aren't so different from those of long-distance running, or anything you do with great purpose. The secret is to stay open and always keep a spirit of curiosity, no matter how proficient you are. "In the beginner's mind there are many possibilities," Suzuki Roshi writes in the prologue. "In the expert's mind there are few."

It was late, but I was so electrified I couldn't sleep. I texted Natalie, I DON'T WANT TO SOUND PRESUMPTUOUS, BUT I FEEL LIKE SUZUKI ROSHI IS INSIDE MY BRAIN!

GOOD, came her reply. KEEP READING.

—

A few days later I go in for a massage. I've been doing strength training all fall, but my left leg is still weaker and sore as it reacclimates to running. My therapist, Wuji, rubs oil onto the scar tissue in my knee, untangling knots of tension, the echoes of injury. I sink into a trance, as I often do on his table, only this time I'm running uphill encased in a drop of water, sloshing gently in my protective bubble. I feel it as much as I see it: the trails and earth, rather than being a force to push against, will absorb me. This is how I will keep my knee safe, running fluidly, without undo force. As though I'm liquid.

Run like the river.

Afterward, I stumble half-conscious from the room. Wuji's waiting for me in the hall with a cup of water. It's that awkward moment when you have to look into the eyes of the person who just ushered you into an out-of-body experience. But Wuji is so woo— he once told me to run "from the bubbling well" of energy coming up through the ground and into my feet—that I'm pretty sure he'll understand. When I tell him what I saw, he bows his head and, like the true shaman he is, whispers, "Wow."

A few days later Natalie stops by. I grab *Zen Mind* from the couch and fling open the front door before she can knock. "Nat!" I cry in mock outrage, holding it up for her to see. "I can't believe we've been friends for seven years, and you've never told me about this book! You've been holding out on me!"

She laughs, pleased, but we both know this isn't entirely true. The seeds of my own hodgepodge Zen practice have been taking root for years: writing and mothering, sitting like a mountain and running like a river. It's only now, though, after breaking my leg, after finding *Zen Mind*, that they're finally beginning to bloom.

—

In the early years after Pippa and Maisy were born and I was just beginning to sit, I learned to count my breaths and release my thoughts like clouds passing in the sky. I sat with other sleep-deprived mothers in empty church rooms and at a mountain Zen center across town where we met once a month to trade in that rarest of commodities—silence—and practice turning even the most frazzling and banal moments of our days into opportunities for mindfulness. I studied briefly with a teacher of indeterminate lineage who declared Zen too rigid for me; I needed something more exuberant, he advised, where I could daydream inside my mind. But I liked the simplicity and austerity of Zen. It balanced the flamboyance of my imagination. I could make Zen wild in my own way. I could sit outside and go very still inside myself and then release it on the mountain and in my notebooks, daydreaming the way I always had: by running and writing.

Sitting taught me how to pay attention without creating stories around what I saw. *Just this is it*, as the Zen saying goes. It brought the world around me into sharper, brighter focus. It was a way of seeing, which made it, paradoxically, a way of writing.

"The most difficult thing is to always keep your beginner's mind. There is no need to have a deep understanding of Zen," Suzuki Roshi wrote. "This is also the real secret of the arts: always be a beginner. Be very careful about this point. It is the secret of Zen practice."

Zen Mind was esoteric and obscure in places, just like Natalie promised, but it was also surprisingly practical. "Zen is not some fancy special art of living," Suzuki Roshi explained. "Our teaching is just to live, always in reality, in its exact sense. To make our effort, moment after moment, is our way." Nor was Zen concerned with banking virtue in this life to cash it in on some blissed-out future existence or simultaneous multiverse. All of life was Zen.

"Whatever you do," he went on, "that is your practice." Like Dogen 800 years before him, Suzuki Roshi believed Zen was rooted in direct experience rather than dogma. It was tactile and facile— right here, right now, eyes open, feet on the ground.

—

Running is simple once again. It requires little more of me than showing up and being patient. There's nothing I want from it now except to be in motion—to move my body on the mountain in order to move my mind. I've always run this way, ever since I was a young girl, but in the years after my father died, running became more complicated. Curious to see how far I could go, I entered races, and won. I wanted to win. I wanted to set records, to be fast. And I wanted my running to be for a greater good, not just for personal gain, but, as Natalie once told me, "for all sentient beings." All my wanting had changed how I felt about running—it was tighter, more constricted, less joyful, more work, not nearly as free.

Anything we do for a long time can become stale if we're not careful. Suddenly there are conditions, demands, desires for recognition, success, profit, improvement. In Zen, this is called "gaining idea," and it's antithetical to zazen. "Our way to sit is not to acquire something; it is to express our true nature," Suzuki Roshi wrote. "That is our practice."

Over time, I'd boxed myself into a rigid definition of success that was nearly impossible to sustain. The more success I enjoyed, the more success I needed to feel good about myself, and the less likely I was to find that success. It was a vicious circle that, if I kept it up, would come to no good end. But my broken leg had broken the cycle. Like it or not, I was a beginner again.

"When we have no thoughts of achievement, no thought of self, we are true beginners," wrote Suzuki Roshi. "Then we can really learn something."

—

I finished *Zen Mind* and began again on page one. I joked to Natalie that reading it was like painting the Golden Gate Bridge: by the time you got to the end, it was time to start over. Surely it contained every secret to being human in the world.

The surgeon still lived in my knee, where he'd taken up residence next to the metal spatula he'd installed, but his voice was getting fainter. I only heard him when it rained and my knee ached, or late at night when the echo of his warning snuck up on me in the vulnerable space between waking and sleeping. Someday, I felt sure of it, I would evict him for good.

My anger was changing, too. It was no longer directed at Steve, or only at Steve. It had a more specific source now, which made it better, but only because things were getting so much worse. Two months earlier, on the first weekend in November, we went to Steve's family reunion on the coast of South Carolina. We fought practically the whole time, not because we were mad at each other, but because we could feel a shadow as big as the land sliding over us. On our last evening there, we stood shoulder to shoulder on a deck overlooking a dock, watching the sun set. I took one final picture, before everything changed—purple light fading like hope from the sky. Then my phone slipped from my hands and with terrible, ominous precision, fell twenty feet through two sets of wooden boards straight into the murky, deep water.

I began to cry, not over my irretrievable phone or because Steve was scolding me for my carelessness, but because it seemed like an awful omen, too glaring to ignore. The next day was Election Day, 2016, and a pall shrouded everything, and the morning after that I woke with dread before dawn and wept for what we'd lost, and would continue to lose—all of us, together, but most especially our daughters.

Now, as winter wore on, the revulsion I'd felt for the plate in my leg was mellowing into mild distaste. I no longer averted my eyes from the lumpy bulge. The scar was four inches long, a pale zipper snaking up my leg like the fine stitches my mother sewed into my torn stuffed animals when I was little. I could feel the plate through my skin; sometimes I touched it. When I closed my eyes, I almost forgot which leg it was. I no longer feared that running would injure me. Instead, I worried that someday I'd forget how it had healed me.

Running is a relationship, an intimacy we have with our body and mind, with the natural world, the weather and mountains, with the people we love at home and those we meet along the way. I couldn't go back to the relationship I'd had; I could only go forward into what it was becoming. But I couldn't use Zen to be a better runner. That would be un-Zen. I would just have to live it, absorb it. I would have to *be* it, the same way I would have to *be* running.

17. TEACHERS

Zen is a living wisdom passed down from Buddha across millennia through a long line of enlightened Zen teachers. These old masters were serious business. They didn't teach the Dharma as much as transmit it through their lives and actions. Koans tell the stories of their long-ago awakenings, but they're not parables or riddles with obvious answers or formulas we can copy. They're more like doorways that lead us forward into deeper understanding, often sparking our own realizations.

Teachers can help illuminate the doorways, but it's up to us to find our own way through. Once, during a formal interview, or *dokusan*, after a daylong retreat, I asked the teacher if it was normal to feel anxious after zazen. He fixed me with a serious gaze and answered with his own koan: "Make sure your thumbs are in the proper position."

The old masters talk to each other through koans, Dharma conversations that span centuries. Each person who studies a koan, touches it and is touched by it, keeps the teaching and the teacher alive. Like all stories, koans are a kind of time travel, filled with secret contents from other eras, waypoints that lead from one teacher to the next, on and on down the line, until they are talking to us.

The more I ran and read *Zen Mind*, the more drawn I was to those long-ago monks seeking enlightenment at the edge of the wild. I wanted real Zen, hardcore Zen, Zen that faced the suffering and uncertainty of life head-on rather than trying to sugarcoat it. Not secular mindfulness or self-help, but badass, ancient-monk Zen. The gloom I felt hovering over us in November had settled in for the long haul: times like these called for the Teachings, capital T.

The problem was, I didn't have a teacher. Well, I did. Suzuki Roshi was my teacher, but he was dead.

Life has an uncanny way of working itself out. You can search a long time for something, only to discover that it's right in front of you.

One day, scrolling through podcasts on my phone, I found Katagiri Roshi. There, between the women's wellness shows and the vegan–ultra runner pods, his elfin face beamed brightly from a stamp-size black and white photograph. He wore black robes and a mischievous smile. I did a doubletake. Natalie's teacher, who'd been dead for thirty years, had a podcast! The show, produced by the Minnesota Zen Center, featured hundreds of archived talks Katagiri Roshi gave there in 1980s. I'd been searching "Zen Dharma talks" for weeks and now here he was, leaping time. Like magic.

I clicked on the first episode. A voice came on, thin and high for a man's, animated. Katagiri sounded very far away. He sounded alive.

I listened, rapt. Every ninth or tenth word I lost to his Japanese accent or the digitized recording, which echoed slightly as though he had been speaking through a rusty tin can. Was he saying "death" or "dots?"

I took Katagiri with me when I walked around our neighborhood after dinner and when I ran up Atalaya before breakfast. The usual structure of time dissolved as I listened. It was winter, or was it spring? The plum trees were blooming but also snow was falling. Neighbors had hung twinkly holiday lights on the branches, and the wet fresh flakes clumped upon them, sparkling like candles on a birthday cake. Was it now or then or some unknown day in the future? Who could say? I was inside the moment and outside of time.

Katagiri talked about how not to conceptualize your life but rather be in it, right in the middle of the stream of time unfolding.

When we live this way, we are in sync with our lives. Another word for this, he explains, is oneness.

Blue jays screeched in the background of Katagiri's warbled recording. Above me, ravens drew circles in the sky with their black wings. Katagiri made a joke and laughed. Natalie had told me he was funny. He was telling the story of a time he flew on an airplane from Minneapolis to San Francisco—if you are not in time with your life, he said, you cannot ride on the plane. You would not get to California. You have to completely be on the plane and be one with the plane, reading the magazine, drinking the champagne. He chuckled, and I could hear the muffled sounds of others' laughter. There were people in the room, in 1988, listening to a Buddhist monk joke about drinking champagne, just as I was listening to him, thirty years later, as I ran up the mountain. In the background, the birds of St. Paul chirped their songs, no longer in this world but somehow still *of* this world. Just like Katagiri.

Sometimes the recording buzzed and Katagiri Roshi's words were difficult to grasp. Other times, his voice was clear but his message was indecipherable. I listened anyway, not trying to understand but simply absorbing what he said into my legs and mind. Sometimes I got to the top of Atalaya and found myself surprised to have gotten there. Had I run or been transported?

Occasionally I gasped out loud because what he said matched exactly how I felt as I ran, and I realized I'd stopped thinking of Katagiri as dead, as no longer alive, because, in some strange way I couldn't explain, he wasn't. He was speaking to me now.

I texted Natalie to tell her I'd found him. KATAGIRI HAS A POD-CAST! HE'S IN MY EARS!

WHAT? she wrote back. HOW CAN I LISTEN? He was her beloved, long-lost teacher, after all. The one who'd changed the course of her life, and in some weird, ricocheting way, mine, too. She'd never listened to podcasts and hadn't known the recordings existed.

For a moment, I wasn't sure, either: *Did* they really exist, or had I imagined them? (Some years later, I will open Katagiri's podcast again, and all but five of his talks will have vanished without a trace, just as mysteriously as they'd appeared.) The next day, Natalie texted back. She'd found him and figured out how to download the recordings onto her phone. I LOVE TO THINK OF YOU RUNNING WITH KR! she wrote, using her shorthand for her great teacher. I CAN'T BELIEVE I'M HEARING HIM AGAIN!

So that's how I thought of him after that. Just Kr and me, running up the mountain.

—

Now I had two dead Zen masters, though the Dharma kept them both a little bit alive. I wondered if I should find a real-life, living, breathing teacher I could meet face-to-face, someone to help tame my rogue practice and make me more assiduous, more proper in my study of the way. I asked Natalie about it. "No," she said flat-out, assuming I meant her, though I hadn't, at least not consciously. "I'm your friend, not your teacher."

The teacher-student relationship is a formal arrangement in Zen with protocols and ceremonies, not one to be entered into lightly. I had a healthy distrust of authority, and organized religion was a major turnoff. Growing up, I dreaded church: the Episcopal services were unspeakably tedious and seemed to have nothing whatsoever to do with my life in the bland, grassy suburbs of New Jersey in the 1980s, with my brown poodle and the blue bicycle I rode everywhere. The only saving grace was my mother's voice—high and bright, clarion. I loved to sit beside her in the pew, smelling her perfume and her suede boots and listening to her sing.

Even other Eastern and Buddhist traditions, with their almost fanatical reverence for gurus, made me nervous. I knew people who went to caves in India, looking for a wizened holy man to answer their most vexing and profound questions.

Teachers were tricky business, even Suzuki Roshi said so. "The moment you meet a teacher, you should leave the teacher," he advised, "and you should be independent." If you become too attached to their way, you risk losing yours. I didn't want a guru or a sage or a zany old monk to smack me with a broom. I already had teachers: mountains and rivers and running and writing. What I really wanted was someone to talk to, someone who would listen to my notions and tell me some of theirs, who made me laugh and steadied me with their presence.

It had been dawning on me slowly for months—like a head trauma victim waking up after a decade in a coma or someone who'd had cotton stuffed in their ears for so long they forgot it was there: I *knew* someone like that. Our arrangement had been formalized for years, right in my very own house.

You don't find a Zen teacher, someone once told me. Your teacher finds you.

A month before I met Steve, in the summer of 2000, I made a list of qualities I was looking for in a partner. I'd spent the year getting over a bad breakup and had more or less made peace with living on my own with my new puppy in my upside-down ship house. I wasn't looking for a boyfriend or mooning over Joan's prediction that I'd meet someone, which, I realized only later, meant I was ready to meet someone. I sat on the porch swing and opened my notebook.

Funny, I wrote at the top of the list, the very first entry. *Good sense of humor.*

I did not have to think about what came next.

Athletic, outdoorsy, good-looking.

It would be nice if he could fix things, like mountain bikes (mine), when they broke.

Of course, kind. *Sweet.*

There must have been other items on the list, but these are the ones I remember, so clearly that when I saw Steve walking toward me across the field a few weeks later, I thought for a second that I must have dreamed him into being.

—

Steve's Zen practice is fly-fishing. He goes almost every week, to the Rio Grande or the Rio Chama, and spends the day casting for

browns and rainbows, working the shoreline without even stopping to eat a sandwich. He throws every fish he catches back into
the river. Sometimes he goes with his friend, Chris, and they pretend they are not competing to see who catches the most fish, but
when I ask Steve, he always knows who won that day.

On winter evenings Steve lies on the couch in his faded khaki
canvas work pants and plaid shirt, watching fly-fishing videos on
his phone. The fishing line hisses as it unfurls on his screen, a high-
pitched whirring when it's reeled back in. The burble of moving
water is delicious on a dark, snowy night in early December.

I lean over his screen. A tiny angler is thigh-deep in a green
river, casting for trout. *"Oooh yeah,"* the angler whispers. It always
impresses me what lengths people will go to, to do what they love.

"I'm in withdrawal already," Steve laments. It's been six days
since he last went fishing. Sometimes I feel like I live in a country
song about beer and fishing and men who have to choose between
their wife and these things.

I'm not always sure which Steve would choose.

I should be clear: Steve's an atheist. A recovering Catholic, he does
not believe in God or *anything*. (From Suzuki Roshi: "I discovered that it is necessary, absolutely necessary, to believe in nothing.") Steve is way more action than talk. He has the maddening,
uncanny ability to worry about almost nothing in the future. He
cares little for image or fame. He never posts on social media. In the
words of one ancient Zen master, he's just "sitting there not influ-
encing anyone." He expends no energy on hypotheticals or gossip,
deplores waste and excess, and patiently waits months for his beautiful gardens to bloom.

One morning that winter, I find Steve sitting on the couch in the
sun, drinking coffee and studying his phone. "I can't believe this
story," he says without looking up. The sun is streaming through
the window behind him, backlighting him in a halo. "It's about

that guy who tied helium balloons to his lawn chair and flew to 16,000 feet."

"Hmmm," I murmur, not really listening. This is how we talk to each other after eleven years of marriage, hearing only every fifth or sixth word, the ones that jump out. Ever since the river accident, we argue more than we used to—about money and dishes, cooking and running and fishing. We bicker about everything but rivers. We haven't been on one together since the Middle Fork.

"Wait, *what* guy?" I ask, suspicious now. "When was this?" My husband and the room wobble into focus.

"1981."

I laugh. "And it's just popping up on your feed *now*? That's some algorithm you've got! 'Give this guy the vintage flying lawn chair stories and cat videos!'"

But Steve's not listening. He's telling me the story. "This dude only planned to lift off to sixteen feet and float above the Mojave Desert and then pop a few balloons and glide down to the ground," he explains. "But when he started hearing the sound of jet engines through the clouds, he became a little concerned."

He looks up at me, as though registering this for the first time too, and snorts. "That's a big difference: sixteen feet to 16,000!"

Steve has this thing he does with his forehead, where he shifts the skin up and backward. It looks as though he's raising his eyebrows or wiggling his ears, but he's not; he's wagging his scalp. The gesture suggests just the slightest amusement. You have to work for it with Steve. I love this about him. He does not crack up just to make you feel good or impress the room, but only when he's genuinely amused. He crinkles his forehead when I say something that might be a tad bit funny and he wants to acknowledge my effort, throw me a bone, without actually laughing at my joke.

After the forehead comes his dimple. That's when you know you are getting somewhere. Sometimes he'll do the forehead on demand, just to humor me. "Do it," I'll say, and his scalp will travel its tiny, rumpled migration, backward and forward, and he'll slap his knee and hold his stomach in mock hilarity until we are both laughing hard and for real. These moments are the best part about us because we're not fighting, and as long as we're still laughing, we'll be okay.

—

It was around this time that Steve got a chia pet from a friend. The Incredible Hulk came gift-wrapped in a brown grocery bag, Scotch tape hanging off at sloppy angles, like all his buddies' bro-gags. The Hulk was six inches tall with grotesque, rippling muscles molded into clay and a severe grimace on his face. Steve poured the seeds and some water into the Hulk's clay planter and set him in a south-facing window. Then he stepped back to admire his handi-work. "How long until he blooms?" I asked the professional horti-culturalist of the house.

"Maybe a few days, a week at most," Steve answered. Like all gardeners, he knows that nothing good comes fast or easy.

The first chia sprouts appeared right on schedule, tiny and encouraging, like chartreuse stubble pushing through tiny pores in the Hulk's pottery. Cloaked in tendrils of green, the Hulk looked sweet, elfin even. Steve tended to him carefully, watering him each morning as the coffee brewed and adjusting him just so in the sunny spot at the window. There the Hulk sat, staring longingly through the pane, as though he knew that no matter how ripped with greenery he became, he would never be able to break free of his clay shell. Something about his posture I found terribly sad—there was a stoic resignation to his bearing that troubled me.

"Does the Hulk seem lonely to you?" I asked Steve one morning as he carried him to the sink for water.

Steve cocked his head, considering. "No, Katie," he said. "The Hulk is made of clay."

The Hulk absorbed every ounce of misplaced empathy I had. I was not really sad for the Hulk, but for what? For the shortness of days, the fragility of life? For all the things, lovely and heartbreaking, that go unspoken between people?

Soon the Hulk's tendrils grew in, coiled and thick like a hair shirt or artificial turf at the mini-golf course. I tried to remind myself that it was just a plant, just seeds growing with water and sun as seeds do, but the effect was strangely appalling. Now the Hulk did not seem tragic but menacing. His matted chest hair burst forth from clay pores, untamed and extravagant. I could see plainly what had eluded me until now: the Hulk was vain. He was not staring through the glass pane, but into it, at his own marvelous, flexing reflection.

Each morning when I came into the kitchen, I glanced at the Hulk, half expecting to find that he had shifted positions slightly overnight. His frown now appeared more like a leer, as though I'd caught him in the moment just after he'd been preening, turning this way and that to admire his bulging biceps and chia pelt, fanning out from the planter in a nauseating frenzy. I examined him closely, his impenetrable stare looking into the far distance, and tried to imagine what he might see. Sometimes deer ambled across the hillside; finches swarmed the bird feeder. It was winter, and the sun took forever to heave itself over the mountain, crawl across our floor, and brighten the room.

The Chia Pet Hulk is revolting and vile. He alarms me. I swear he is moving in the night when no one is looking.

I secretly began to wish that the Hulk would die.

He would, of course. It was only a matter of time. The Hulk's chia pelt had become a bush. Soon enough the plant would begin its slow but inevitable decline. Nothing is permanent; suffering is universal. This is the central truth of Buddhism. Not even the invincible chia Hulk was exempt.

There was the question of what to do with the Hulk. When the time came.

"Is it edible?" I asked Steve, vaguely horrified by the idea of for-aging the Hulk's chest hair for salad greens.

There it was again, Steve's scalp, waggling.

"Theoretically, yes."

—

We see in others what we resist in ourselves. The Hulk had arrived in our house as a joke, and in a span of three weeks, I had projected all my love and fear, my compassion and darkness, my sadness and hope onto his fragile terra-cotta carapace. He was, as Steve said, just a lump of clay baked in a kiln in China. Less animate than the fish that swam in our aquarium, swirling through their watery keep, embroiled in secret dramas and unspeakable warfare. (It's a fallacy that fish are peaceful. They fight each other and get fish-warts and STDs and drift sideways when they lose control of their bodies and perish belly-up and alone, only to be plucked out of the water by my husband's gentle, searching hands.)

Steve watched the fish as intently as I watched the Hulk. Sometimes I found him sitting on the bench in the kitchen, lost in thought as he observed their gliding forms. In those moments, I could see him as a blonde-haired boy of seven, the youngest of four, alone in his house, bathed in bluish light, settling his own tur-moil as he skirted the edges of family skirmishes, moving quietly, like a fish, unseen.

We were not our fish, nor were we the Hulk. We were humans raising other, smaller humans in a house with tall ceilings and two dogs and windows that let the light in, trying to face each other and ourselves with clear eyes that didn't turn to stone but saw all the way through to the bright parts inside.

—

The Hulk left us on an otherwise uneventful February day. Steve picked him up from the windowsill, pulled his chia out by the roots, and tossed the whole snarled wad into the compost bin. The clay carapace, lifeless and stripped of Hulk's herbaceous musculature,

Steve stashed unceremoniously in a roundabout cabinet next to the steak knives.

Suddenly I was sad. It was just his form. Zen tells us we are all form and emptiness at the same time, emptiness and form. And yet. The moments we'd had with the Hulk were over, gone in a flash of verdant spouts growing by the millimeter. I knew his type—strong and silent, forehead creased into familiar lines. His sneer no longer seemed so threatening, just a little wistful. What was the Hulk, if not time passing, and far too quickly?

"Do you ever miss the Hulk?" I asked Steve a few days later. He cocked his head, as though actually considering the question, then shook it no. "He's in the cupboard."

I wondered, not for the first time, who this husband of mine was, where he came from and how he became so funny and dry, self-possessed, his very own self, and how I got him, my accidental Zen master. The man who waters a clay Hulk, reads a forty-year-old story of a flying lawn chair held aloft by birthday balloons, and gives himself over to it for many, many minutes in a row, letting it sink in.

All the while inscrutable, saying nothing, just wagging his scalp, smiling with his dimple, while I wish I understood what lies beneath it all.

And yet I do.

I know how Steve feels when he stands on the bank, casting his long looping line in swishing, meditative arcs, why he needs it as much as I need running and sitting and mountains and rivers. And why he loves it so: waiting patiently for a trout to rise and landing it, content to cup it in his hands for an instant before letting it go.

18. FORGETTING

There's a concept in Zen called "no trace." It's like the well-known wilderness ethic: when in nature, we should pack out our trash, cover our tracks, and travel gently, so that we leave minimal physical evidence of having been there. In Zen, the trace refers to our thoughts. When we have ideas of how something should be or how life once was or might someday become, our thoughts leave a trace. A shadow of expectation, a residue of preconceived ideas and judgments, covers our present experience.

"These traces make our minds very complicated," Suzuki Roshi writes in *Zen Mind*. "When we do something with a quite simple, clear mind, we have no notions or shadows, and our activity is strong and straightforward."

It was November 2017, and I was going to run forty-two miles across the Grand Canyon and back in a day. I'd done it once before, four years earlier. That first time, I hadn't cared about my time or if I was running fast and well, which had freed me to run fast and well and to set what I would only later learn was a fastest-known time, or FKT—a women's record that would stand for seven years.

It would be hard to top that day, or to forget it, which I didn't want to, ever. I just couldn't hold on too tightly to the memory, or else I'd make it impossible for myself to go back.

"We should forget, day by day, what we have done," advises Suzuki Roshi. "This is true nonattachment. And we should do something new. To do something new, of course, we must know our past, and this is all right. But we should not keep holding onto anything we have done; we should only reflect on it."

I'd been having a funny feeling about my writing recently, as though my book about my father could be reduced to four words—living, dying, writing, and running—and that maybe it needed nothing more than those four words. Had I written a whole book of words just to come to this point, to see that the stories themselves were tangential? The book existed without me now. It could stand on its own, as those four words. And maybe someday I could stand on it.

I wondered if the same could be true of my running. If it could exist without me. If I could run so deep into the Grand Canyon that I ran beyond myself, leaving no trace. "You must be true to your own way until at last you come to the point where you see it is necessary to forget all about yourself," wrote Suzuki Roshi. It was the best line in *Zen Mind, Beginner's Mind*, its own beautiful, confounding koan: If I could forget myself, would I run faster, without *trying* to run faster?

—

I start before dawn in shorts and a T-shirt and a light jacket. Below me the South Kaibab Trail skewers 4,000 vertical feet in seven miles to the Colorado River. It's forty degrees, but within minutes, I'm sweating feverishly through my wind jacket, heat coming off me in hot, soggy waves. My throat begins to hurt. I've been outrunning a cold all week; now it's caught me.

Every switchback brings me closer to the bottom and farther from the top. I can't stop thinking about how I am going to climb back out. This problem consumes me for a long time. I've run through all sorts of unfavorable conditions—hail, sleet, snow, pain—but I've never run with a fever before. I begin to worry that I have the flu. Not just the flu, but the fatal flu. I will become a statistic and orphan my daughters, all for a stupid run.

I decide I will not make any decisions in the dark. I keep going, waiting for daylight. Eventually the sky is gray enough that I can turn off my headlamp. I can see flashes of the Colorado River far below. I decide I will turn around when I get to the river and run back up to the South Rim so that I don't keel over and die, possibly right there on the trail.

Not dying is always my first goal in running.

When I get to the river, I decide I will cross the black iron bridge and run half a mile to Bright Angel Campground and refill my water from the tap before I turn around.

I feel this is a good plan.

When I get to the tap I look down and right there on the ground beside the spigot, gleaming up at me, are two small, rusty-colored tablets, like cinnamon Red Hots. I squeeze my eyes shut and open them again. Still there. Little glowing jewels in the dirt, positioned perfectly at my feet as though left there just for me.

I bend over and pick them up. They are the exact shape and color of Advil and are branded with a tiny stamp that reads A-2. I decide to pocket them but not eat them—they could be anything! Narcotics or nighttime cold medicine or hallucinogens that might make me pass out or wander lost and deranged through the canyon.

Ahead of me is the fourteen-mile climb to the North Rim. I decide to take off my jacket and run a ways uphill to see if it is the jacket that has been making me so steamy. Even with bare arms and legs, at 7:00 a.m. in the deep shadows of the Inner Gorge, I am dripping and hot.

I keep going, sometimes jogging and sometimes stopping, trying to decide what to do. I convince myself that I can quit now, still chalk up the day as a solid training run, and return to the canyon when I am healthy. I like this idea for about one minute, until I remember it has taken me four years and a broken leg to come back this time.

I keep running because I don't know what else to do.

—

The Inner Gorge is the deepest, oldest part of the deepest canyon on the continent. Geologists call it the basement. The rock is black with age. Two-billion-year-old slabs of Vishnu schist jut out at jagged angles above the river. It is beautiful in the tortured, wizened way of something that has withstood enormous upheaval and near constant change on a scale the human brain cannot comprehend.

I knew something about basements. I'd been in one for several years after my father died. His own, actual basement at his farm in Virginia, where he kept all his photographs and letters and diaries, where, in the aftermath of his death, my grief took on an archeological quality and became an excavation of his life and mine, together. It was the sort of uprooting that unearths things you hadn't known and wished you didn't know but also couldn't not know, and maybe had always, deep down, known.

The basement was also where I had lived above ground, though, when my grief morphed into an irrational fear that I too was dying. This is a special kind of darkness, to live in perpetual dread of your own death. It didn't make sense. I could run for hours, and many days I did. I was almost never dying when I was running. It was the only time I could silence the voices in my head.

My anxiety eventually subsided, but it didn't go away completely. Winter was the worst—the season my father died, when the sun was at its lowest—and I could feel grief coming, slouching in on the shadow of shortening days. I was beginning to understand, even predict, its patterns. I could be in the basement on the top of a mountain, too, in full sun while writing a book about love and secrets and the things I knew but wished I didn't. Even when you can see sixty miles in all directions or are climbing through blooming yucca in a canyon older than time, you might find yourself in the basement.

You can give in to the anxiety or you can keep going. This is the secret to surviving the basement: you almost always have a choice, even when you feel like you don't.

—

Somehow I make it seven more miles to Cottonwood Campground, halfway to the North Rim. Two hikers are filling their water bottles from a spigot. I stagger up to them, my throat so scratchy I can barely form words. I pull the dirty red pills from my pocket and hold them up in my grimy palm for them see. "I found these on the ground," I say. "Do you know what they are?"

The men exchange pitying glances. One reaches wordlessly into his backpack and fishes out a Ziplock bag full of identical red tablets, right down to the inscription, A-2. He must have one hundred of them, at least. "Advil, 200 milligrams," he says, holding it out for me. It's mesmerizing, almost obscene, how many he has. I must be staring because the man says, "Do you want some of ours? They're clean."

I shake my head. "No, I'm good." Pause, reconsider. "Actually, I'm not good. I'm sick. But now that I know what these are, I'm going to take them. Then I'm going to make the hard call and turn around."

I make a big show of licking the two pills from my hand into my mouth and swallowing them with a gulp of water. They leave tiny red, blotchy pill prints on my palm. The men watch me with a sad fascination, but to me it seems completely rational to decline their Advil and eat the dirty ones I'd picked up off the ground instead.

Clearly I'm beyond hope, so they say, "Good luck!" and begin walking uphill away from me. I sit on the bench and watch them go and try to psych myself up to give up. I eat an orange. I read the information sign telling me it is still seven miles and 4,600 vertical feet to the North Rim. I know beyond a doubt that there is absolutely no way I will be able to run there in my condition.

I was never dying when I was running, but this time I might be.

—

Two women trot by, on their way down from the North Rim. They look so fresh and purposeful. I decide to use their energy. Energy is contagious, and I can borrow some of theirs. I get up immediately and follow them back down the trail, the way I'd come. Their ponytails are bouncy and clean, and I focus on them as I run. I make it maybe five steps and then I stop. I can't do it. I just can't.

I turn around and start jogging uphill in the direction of the North Rim. I feel better for having made a decision, however flawed and foolhardy, but there is the problem of the men. What will I tell them when I catch up to them? What possible explanation can I give for continuing? The shame I feel is almost enough to make me want to turn around again.

Almost.

Then, there they are, about to cross the wooden footbridge over Roaring Springs.

I pick up speed, trying to look peppy, and pass the men on my left, forcing cheer into my voice as I call over my shoulder, "Just giving the Advil a chance to kick in!"

It must, because I am able to jog most of the next four miles, through the steepest section, where the trail—barely three feet wide—is bordered on one side by sheer limestone walls and the other by a 2,000-foot vertical drop.

Do not fall, I tell myself sternly.

Mommy, I whisper.

The ponderosa pines on the North Rim gradually get closer. Surprisingly, I am still capable of rational observations: my lungs are scorched and my breath raspy, but I have no pain in my legs or knees. Also, I am not puking—a hopeful sign. Maybe I am not going to die today after all! I am well hydrated, and the weather is clear and stable. I decide right then and there that if anything changes for the worse—even one thing—I will turn around immediately.

Immediately.

I walk the final mile to the North Rim. It is 11:00 a.m. and I still have twenty-two miles to go, back the exact same way I'd come. A woman at the trailhead waves at me and frowns, "You don't look so great," she said. "Do you need something, a soda, maybe?"

I nod sheepishly and follow her to her truck, where she rifles through the backseat and produces a bag of potato chips and a Dr. Pepper. I would have taken anything from anyone in that moment, without hesitation, chugging it right down, no questions asked. I drink half the soda while she takes a selfie of us. "Are you famous?" she asks. I see from the picture that I have a crazed look in my eye, but shortly afterward I begin to perk up. I've never had a soda during a run before. If nothing else comes from this day, I think, at least I'll have learned that I can drink a Dr. Pepper while running and it will save me.

After about two miles down, though, I become frightened again. The sugar and caffeine have worn off, and nothing has ever looked so far away as the South Rim does from this vantage, just a high purple smudge on the distant horizon. I stare down at the trail skirting the canyon's edge. I will never make it. It is too far and so exposed. I want to sit down in the dirt and give up, but where will that get me? I'd still be stuck in this stupid canyon.

Just make it to Cottonwood, I tell myself.

When I get to Cottonwood, I refill my water and sit on the bench and eat my last orange.

I decide I will buy another soda at Phantom Ranch. This thought keeps me going for seven miles.

Just make it to the river, I tell myself.

It takes forever to get to the river, and when I finally lurch into the canteen, sweaty-faced and filthy, there's only lemonade. I buy a cup and run back to the trail, holding it in my hand and drinking as I go, like a waiter at a cocktail party.

Much of the South Kaibab Trail is too steep to run, even on a good day. I slow to a power hike, bent over, hands on thighs. You'd think it would feel good to hike after running for so long, but it doesn't. It feels worse, much worse. For seven miles I trudge as fast as I can uphill, bracing my aching lower back with my hands, too tired and lazy to eat, mentally flicking my middle finger at the canyon. I am done with it and with ultra running, forever.

Just get to the South Rim. Then you'll never have to do this ever again.

The river is getting farther away, and I can see less of it. I jog very slowly through whatever sections I can, one switchback at a time. The South Kaibab is steepest at the top, and at last I see it narrowing into a tiny chute through tight switchbacks. I round one and then another. I start crying, big gulping gasps of air through my echoey chest. It hurts to cry. I run the last switchback, passing two hikers, up through a little slot in the dirt and throw myself onto the rim, sobbing from disbelief, fatigue, relief. "I did it, I did it, I did it," I cry out loud, not caring that the hikers are staring at me.

I pull out my phone. It's 4:17 p.m.

It has taken me ten hours and thirty-six minutes, an hour and fifteen minutes slower than last time, so far off my record, but I'd let go of that hours earlier.

It had been very stubborn of me to continue all that way.

I am ashamed that I had.

I can never, ever tell my mother.

Still, the most important thing is that I hadn't died. It will take time to sort out what happened in the canyon, if it had been a good idea to continue, or a terrible one, and why I did.

—

Back in Santa Fe, I told Natalie the whole story. I expected her to scold me gently, but instead she said, "Oh, that's true Zen. You just kept going."

It didn't seem Zen to me, it seemed reckless and dumb, but I knew what she meant. She was talking about great determination, continuing onward without becoming deterred by difficulties or details, bad weather or attitude, preferences or positions. As Dogen famously wrote, "Fearing the swift passing of the sunlight, practice the way as though saving your head from fire."

But continuing in the Zen way doesn't mean going forward blindly, masochistically, leaving your body in the dirt to die. It requires prudence and equanimity. In some circumstances it may mean stopping so you can get up the next day and do it again. You don't have to believe in Zen to have a Zen spirit, to have patience and endurance.

I knew all this and still I suspected I should have stopped.

Nat was giving a Dharma talk at the Zen center in a few days and asked if she could tell my story. "This is exactly what my talk is about: going up the mountain is the same as going down!"

Before I went to the Grand Canyon, I would have told her this was silly. Going up is totally different. Everyone knows this. It's harder. And going down is easier, faster. You can let gravity carry you. But now I understood it was nothing like that. Really, they are the same. You have to go all the way down, and then you have to climb out. You can't say one is better, the other worse, one is bad, the other good. The same is true for running or not running, for starting and stopping, feeling sick or feeling well. Winning or losing. You meet a thing head on and do it.

Whatever it is.

"When you do something, you should do it with your whole body and mind," Suzuki Roshi wrote. "You should do it completely, like a good bonfire. You should not be a smoky fire…. Zen activity is an activity which is completely burned out, with nothing remaining but ashes."

I'd thought it was my ego that kept me going. But maybe I *had* run beyond myself, so far that I left my body behind. I'd been a muddled, indecisive, bawling mess, but even so, the activity—the running itself—had been strong and straightforward. I'd gone across the canyon and back. I'd burned it all down to ashes. It had been nothing like I imagined—a transcendence that felt exactly like obstinance. To release it all, I'd had to carry it all: the grubby Advil and my creeping terror and shame and the energy of the women with bouncy ponytails and the icy lemonade, the anxiety I couldn't shake and the feeling that I was younger than any of it and older than I'd ever been.

19. UNDOING

Two months pass in the pages of a notebook, fall switching over to winter. One December morning, as I run up the mountain, leaving footprints in the melting slush of an early storm, echoes of words come back to me: *I will run one hundred miles*. I'd written them in the red notebook a year and a half earlier, after Idaho, when I was dreaming my way into healing. *I will run through wildflowers. Maybe Leadville.*

Each August, the small mining town of Leadville, Colorado, hosts back-to-back hundred-mile mountain bike and trail running races. When I was in my late twenties in Santa Fe and rode my mountain bike everywhere, I imagined someday competing in the storied Leadville 100 race. But I never signed up: the idea of grinding out nine hours on my bicycle in a single day—and hundreds more in training—intimidated me. I met Steve, got married, had babies, and let the dream go.

But now here it is again, Leadville: sputtering to the surface, startlingly obvious.

Oh. Yes.

That night I go on the internet. The Leadville Trail 100 Run is among the largest and most challenging hundred-mile ultramarathons in the country, longer than I've ever run. Made famous in part by the 2010 best-selling book *Born to Run*, Leadville is so popular that entry is by random drawing. Of the many thousands of people who put their name into the lottery, only about 800 are chosen at random. I check the calendar. The deadline for applying to the drawing is the following week. There's no cost to enter; the race fee of 400 dollars will only be charged if my name is selected.

Beside me, Steve is a hibernating bear sprawled out on the couch, fast asleep under the living room lights. I tap my name and credit card number into the online form, type a few words explaining why I want to run the race: *recovering from accident* and *broken leg*. My odds are long, and the race is so far away—next August—that none of what I do next feels real.

Okay? The button blinks at me, question and answer both.

I hit Okay.

—

A few weeks later, Steve and I left the girls with friends and went to a small cabin in a remote valley with a little river running through it. It was supposed to be peaceful, just the two of us, but I cried because I missed the girls, and Steve and I fought because I was ruining everything with my crying.

The crying itself wasn't new—I'd been crying since I fell out of the raft, since my father died, since our babies were born. Crying from love and wonder and joy as much as from fear and grief and the news of the world. But this crying scared me. It felt different, like the thing beneath my worry, a dark and pocked pit at the very bottom of my soul, ridged and full of grooves where scary thoughts got stuck. These tears were not particular or circumstantial but almost primordial, as though they'd sprung from the deepest part of me and also beyond me.

It made me think of the Zen koan that asks, "What is your original face before even your parents were born?" The sorrow felt that old. Mine but also not-mine.

I sat on the porch beside the stream, my husband somewhere upstream diligently working its banks, and felt a tremendous sadness well up in me. There were so many ways of being. What if the way I'd picked was wrong? A ragged sob came up from my belly and escaped my mouth.

I thought of the woman who owned the cabin where we were staying. That morning, she'd ridden up on a horse to see if we needed anything. Her brown hair was pulled back low against her neck; the ends were tangled by the wind. She'd come to this valley ten years ago by chance, fell in love, and never left. It was not the life she'd pictured for herself, she admitted, but it was the one she chose. "Moment after moment we have to find our own way," Suzuki Roshi wrote in *Zen Mind, Beginner's Mind*. "Some idea of perfection or some perfect way which is set up by someone else is not the true way for us."

I waited on the cabin steps for a long time, as the sun grazed the treetops, watching for Steve to come loping back through the meadow with his fly rod over his shoulder. I could picture his shape exactly, like the first time I saw him—walking out of my imagination and into my life.

All this time, I'd been a carpenter, hammering and patching the broken parts of myself back into something recognizable, but I was still just a loosely assembled collection of bones covered in skin, empty on the inside.

—

A woman I once met told me that shortly after she turned forty, she experienced what she described as a strange instinct to go farther and deeper. "I thought of it as an undoing," she explained, an unraveling of her structured life of convention, a physical urge to move beyond the routines she'd built for herself. It came out when she walked, sometimes hours every day, in the hills and trails outside Denver, where she lived.

"Every time I go out walking, I just want to keep going."

I knew what she meant. It was why I ran for dozens of miles and many hours at once. I was building something—toiling in the deepest, loneliest, moldiest basement, writing, while I ran along the tops of mountains. Dirty and chalky with dust, I strung together words to make sentences, and steps to make miles, going farther into wilderness and deeper into the landscape of my imagination.

Did I want this still? Some days I couldn't say.

I had made a book, constructed it out of my notebooks and the air and the trees and the dirt while I ran, and memories, secrets, broken promises, broken bones. I was making another book now, too—this one—the story just beginning to reveal itself in my pages, stitching itself into the shape of something I couldn't yet grasp. All I could think of was the Zen koan that asks, so simply, "What is this?"

—

It was early January, the darkest, hardest, coldest time of year, but the only thing I wanted was to run. I put on a billion layers and drove ten miles down a washboard road to the Rio Grande. The canyon was wide and bright, the river marching along—winter-clear, undisturbed. I ran with it, downstream, below crumbling basalt cliff bands, and then began to climb a steep, rough trail to the rim. Downstream, I could see the bend in the river where we'd sheltered in the willows years earlier with the girls when a sudden thunderstorm hit. I could see the twists our lives had taken, were still taking.

There's a famous Zen story that tells of Dogen's path to enlightenment. He first tasted impermanence as a grieving child of eight, watching incense smoke drift into the air at his mother's funeral. When he was thirteen, he became a monk; at twenty-five, he left for China to seek the way. It was there, late at night in a darkened temple, upon hearing his older master declare, "Zen is the shedding of body and mind," that he had his first great awakening. This became the bedrock of his Zen philosophy. "To study the Buddha Way is to study the self," he famously wrote in the *Genjo Koan*. "To study the self is to forget the self and become actualized by myriad things."

Katagiri Roshi sometimes spoke about cliff divers who flung themselves into the ocean from unfathomable heights. He described their arcing backs and the way they both rise through the air and curve toward the ocean at the same time—a dazzling, peculiar alchemy. This is beauty, he said, not because their bodies are beautiful and muscled, though they are, and not because they are doing something tremendously daring, though this is certainly true, but because they are moving in unison with the energy of the cliff and the air, the water, their own minds and bodies, and even time itself.

They have entered the stream of life, what Kr called the "dynamic functioning of the universe." This is flow.

The same is true of mountain climbers or piano players, sailors, actors, basketball players, and runners, of people driving cars or flying on airplanes, of anyone who participates fully and with total devotion to the activity of their life. The important point is to be open and flexible, elastic, so that your body and mind can become one. When you do, you yourself disappear and "become completely zero," creating what Kr called "a beautiful form." You may not always recognize this, but other people can feel it.

This was how I felt when I ran: that I was touching something beyond me that didn't have words but was a feeling, a momentum greater than my own but part of me, too. Inside of me and outside of me at the same time. The form I created with my body in running was in part functional; it was how I moved through space and time. Yet it was also beyond form. It was energy, creativity.

I thought I'd withered my soul in the basement, chasing darkness, but really I'd been pouring the mountains, the sky, the rivers, into words, into the world.

—

Did I still want to run far and deep? Yes, but there was something else now, too. I wanted to strip myself bare. I wanted to peel back layers, pare away the superfluous, just as my accident had.

After his awakening, Dogen returned from China. He did not carry with him the idea of enlightenment. Even that he set down. "I have returned to my native country with empty hands. There is not even a hair of Buddhism in me. Now I pass the time naturally. The sun rises in the east every morning, and the moon sets in the west. When the clouds clear, an outline of the mountains appears, and as the rain passes away, the surrounding mountains bend down. What is it, after all?"

20. FORM

The email arrives one night after dinner in mid-January 2018. It has been eighteen months since my accident, a year since I'd started running again and found *Zen Mind, Beginner's Mind*.

CONGRATULATIONS! it reads. YOU HAVE BEEN SELECTED FOR THE LEADVILLE TRAIL 100 RUN. I'm so surprised, I yelp. "Oh my God, I got into Leadville!" Steve and the girls look up from their books, as startled as I am. They can't tell if this is good news or not—my tone is not one of pure elation; it holds the unique horror, too, of realizing I got what I wanted and now have to do it.

I stare at the email until the words swim in my eyes and feel like tears, but aren't. Or maybe they are. One hundred miles, farther than I've ever run. Do I want to? Is it even possible? It's January. August is a million years away.

—

I can't remember the running as much as the sitting, at least in the beginning. It seemed like all I did was sit, though surely that isn't true.

I hadn't shaken the sadness I'd felt a few weeks earlier at the cabin. My worry as I knew it was swift and capricious, but this gloom had a heavy, stolid mass. Maybe it had been there all along and had only just begun to rise to the surface, like a rotten tire or waterlogged stump that sunk before bobbing slowly from the depths. To shove it back under would only make it worse. It would come up someplace else, danker and smellier. I had to face it straight on.

Sitting, like running, has its own form. Suzuki Roshi espoused a simple, if precise, method passed down from Dogen: upright spine, eyes open and downcast, thumbs and fingertips clasped loosely at the navel in the shape of an oval. "The most important thing is to own your own physical body," Suzuki Roshi explains in *Zen Mind,*

Beginner's Mind. "If you slump, you will lose yourself. Your mind will be wandering about and you will not be in your body. This is not the way! We must exist right here, right now!"

The old master sounded strict, but if you looked closely, you could find loopholes. "Doing something is expressing our own nature," he went on. "The purpose of these rules is not to make everyone the same, but to allow each to express their own self more freely." It was far better to demonstrate the spirit of determination than to fret about flawless form. Like Dogen before him, Suzuki Roshi believed that zazen is not a means of attaining enlightenment, but an expression of enlightenment. Each of us is already awakened. We don't have to be perfect, all we have to do is make sincere effort and be ourselves.

I wanted to try another streak—a sitting streak. I wanted to see if I could meditate every day for a month. I would not measure time. I could sit for two minutes and it would count. I could sit for two breaths. Everything counted. I wanted to see if I could stay with the dark moments the way I stayed with my fears in the Grand Canyon, to go deep into them before climbing out.

I wondered if by making myself more vulnerable, I would become less vulnerable.

A few minutes here and there, six or eight at a time. I rarely increased the duration or bothered to try. I'd been telling myself the same story for years, ever since I learned to meditate: I was a runner, and sitting still didn't come naturally to me.

Then one day I met a friend of Natalie's who was visiting from California. I told Bill my theory, and he barked with laughter.

"That's exactly why you should be able to sit for a long time! *Because* you've trained yourself to run for a long time!"

I cocked my head. Hmmm. I'd never looked at it that way.

And then: Shoot, I thought. I'd gotten it backward. Bill was right. I had no excuses.

These thoughts were followed swiftly by relief. I had the skills to sit. Maybe I was born to sit.

It was almost a revelation.

After that, I just sat. No expectations. I sat in front of the woodstove before bed, in the dark of early morning before the girls and Steve got up, before I climbed the mountain on skis or in sneakers and the snow clung to the trees like meringue and the clouds hung above the Rio Grande Valley, parting now and then to reveal the curved brown contours of town slowly waking up to the day.

Some days it was peaceful—two minutes, soft breath in the quiet night house—and my mind was like a cork floating atop my body, light and airy, and there was no static, no sharp charge of fear bolting through me. I was a piece of bark bobbing in the soft ocean. Other days I wanted to scream and get up after five seconds. I sat on my shabby zafu after breakfast, before bed, outside in the bright, brittle winter mornings, and in the living room, in the middle of a temper tantrum, to keep from yelling back.

> *Day fifteen—eight minutes in the heat of resistance and*
> *P's howling fit about her science fair project.*
> *I have to be the grown-up.*
> *I am the grown-up.*

"You should not be tilted sideways, backwards, or forwards," instructs Suzuki Roshi, but on the days when I flopped over onto the floor, I lay where I fell like a murder victim, sobbing softly into the carpet. Really, I began to realize, I was just sad or ashamed or angry—all the standard human emotions we do our best to avoid.

Sitting with them, and sometimes buckling under them, was painful, but when I did, I could see them and name them, and when I named them, I could see they weren't me but rather wily stowaways, hobos hopping a train, trying to hitch a ride on my heart. I didn't need to carry them if I didn't want to.

—

My energy for sitting was building, as though a hole in me had opened and could only be filled by sitting. The more I sat, the more I thought about sitting and wanted to sit. I sat on mountain summits for a moment after I ran to the top, and I sat beside the little river near our house on frosty winter mornings, after bike-riding the girls to school, breathing in time with the swoosh of the current.

I signed up for a daylong retreat at the Zen center. The first sitting period was fifty minutes, interminable, an ultramarathon of meditation. But plenty of people sit this long, or longer; I knew enough about Zen to know it wasn't all that special, and if you thought it was, you still had work to do. Lots of work. It's like running long distances—eventually, you just have to go for it.

I counted my breaths in and out and focused my gaze on a fuzzy glint of light on the dark wood floor. I had many thoughts about sitting, about my knee and tendons, about Steve and the girls, where they were and if they were safe. But I just sat, didn't fight or follow my thoughts as I so often had. "Do not try to stop your mind, but leave everything as it is," Suzuki Roshi had written. "Things will come as they come and go as they go. Then eventually your clear, empty mind will last fairly long."

I sat and sat and felt able and very still, and it was only in the final ten minutes that my legs and hips and shins began to ache so that I longed to move and for the bell to ring and to resent it for not ringing. But I did not shift or move and I kept breathing quietly and counting my breaths until at last it did.

Afterward, I got up and walked out, moving with a strange languor that felt exaggerated but was not. Deep, smooth breaths filled my body and all my movements seemed distinct, slowed down, cinematic. Outside, a magpie sat on the viga beam of the zendo, iridescent black with a pure white strip sweeping across its breast. It perched silently and then issued a high shrill screech and took wing, prowling the fallow garden beds and hoop houses before coming to rest on a juniper tree.

I thought about the story of the bird that had built a nest on Buddha's head as he meditated. The Buddha sat for seven years. Was it hyperbole, myth? Magic?

The bird in that story was a magpie.

"Do not think that time merely flows away," Dogen wrote in his famous essay, "Uji, The Time Being," in 1240. "The time-being has the quality of flowing. So-called today flows into tomorrow, today flows into yesterday, yesterday flows into today."

Maybe it had really been three minutes, but it felt like seven years. Or maybe it was seven years but passed like three minutes. Or, as Steve jokes each summer when we celebrate our wedding anniversary: "It feels like ten minutes . . . underwater!"

We are not separate from time, we are time.

In the story, the Buddha blinked and saw the morning star shimmering in the sky; in that moment, he and all beings were awakened.

In Santa Fe, the magpie flew away.

Sitting felt real and alive in me, independent of conditions and outcome. I didn't talk about it. I just did it.

It reminded me of running, something I knew I would do for a long time, perhaps my whole life, and so there was no urgency, no reason to clutch or demand things from it. I couldn't have said why I felt this way, but it wasn't a sign of ambivalence; rather the opposite. It didn't require words or explanation. It reminded me of falling in love.

Five minutes here, ten minutes there, breathing, flopping, twitching, crying, until January was over and I had done it, I had straggled through my month-long streak. The commitment I made to sitting seeped into and became indistinguishable from the commitment I'd made to Leadville.

—

On the first warmish morning in late February, I go outside to meditate beside the fountain. I wear my down jacket with the hood pulled over my head and carry my notebook in one hand and a coffee mug in the other. I settle onto my cushion. It is as shabby and faded as ever, but now I see it differently: my poor disheveled zafu *is* Zen. Everything is Zen when you see it clearly for what it is, rather than what you want it to be.

I take a sip of coffee, hot and bitter. The mug had been hand-painted by a friend of my father's; a jaunty red fox dashes across the ceramic glaze. Suddenly I'm transfixed, filled with an almost unbearable tenderness for the mug: it is inert but alive, smooth, substantial, imbued with mystery and an energy all its own. The fact of its existence, and of my drinking from it, could alter something in the world—the writing I am doing in this book. It could become this book.

But how? It's odd and abstract, and yet I am full of the idea, and the idea is full in me. The realization that the mug alters this moment, imperceptibly but undeniably, and by extension the world, does not strike me as fanciful but fundamentally accurate. Each action, no matter how mundane, affects another, on and on down the line, forever.

I can hold the mug, and this will change something; though there might never be any trace of the changing, it will have happened. It's real. I feel the day open around me. The mug is connected to everything, just like the dog barking across the arroyo, just like Kr and his birds, like Sharon, a woman I knew who will die of breast cancer, and like the black rock splitting the river.

Nothing is left out. They are all part of this story, and this story is part of everything.

21. RIGHT EFFORT

One hundred miles is inconceivable. The longest I've run since my accident was forty-two miles across the Grand Canyon and back with the flu, which still occasionally struck me as so profoundly idiotic I wasn't sure if it even counted.

Now when I think about Leadville, sparks of terror shimmer through my brain. I think about the surgeon: "If I were you, I'd find a new hobby." I think about my knee calcifying into a giant blob of arthritis. I think about how I probably ought to run less and be home more. But then I decide I can't think about one hundred miles, whether I am doing it right or getting it all wrong. I just have to run.

Ultra running has grown and changed a lot since I ran my first 50k in 2012. There are more races and more people running them; many ultramarathons now sell out months in advance or, like Leadville, use a lottery system to limit entries. There is more gear, more apps, more coaches to help you optimize your performance. More hacks and supplements and recovery tools. More data. So much data it makes my head hurt.

I don't want more from running, though. I want less: I want simplicity and ease. I want the air and sky and birds and the ideas in my head. I want running itself. If zazen is just sitting, I want just running. I've always been old school this way. I don't have a coach. I rarely track my miles or speed, I don't do structured workouts. I want to run the way I used to: free.

My plan for Leadville is the same: no plan. Practically speaking, I'll gradually increase the length of my runs by a few miles each week and move as much as possible every day. Between walking the girls to school and running and walking the dog after dinner, I can cover about fifteen miles a day. I once heard that the most important metric in training for one hundred miles isn't weekly mileage or pace but time on your feet. I make this my mantra. I will get used to moving all day, running on tired legs, staying in motion.

How do you train for one hundred miles? The same way you heal a broken leg: you listen. Do your legs want to go faster? Do they need to rest? Is your heart heavy? Do you even feel like running? I become a close observer of my moods: Are my legs springy when I wake in the morning, or are they encased in cement? Do I tear out the door because I can't wait to go up the mountain, or do I stall, inventing a dozen dumb chores to do before I leave the house?

My only training guide isn't a running book but *Zen Mind, Beginner's Mind*—in particular, a dog-eared chapter called "Right Effort." Right effort, Suzuki Roshi explains, is pure practice, untainted by desire for achievement or attainment, gain or fame. It is pursuing an activity with the appropriate amount of energy and intensity, not going overboard or being melodramatic, not making a big show out of it, but devoting yourself to your practice thoughtfully, persistently.

"When you make some special effort to achieve something, some excessive quality, some extra element is involved," he writes. "You should get rid of excessive things." Right effort is sustainable, continuous effort—something you can do for days, months, years, a lifetime.

—

In 2002, after we'd been together for two years, Steve and I went to Nepal. I'd wanted to go to Mount Everest since 1996, when I'd researched a magazine story about an infamous storm that killed eight climbers while they descended from the summit. This article later became the basis of John Krakauer's best-selling book *Into Thin Air.* I'd developed a frightful fascination with the inhospitable rock pile on the south side of Everest that turned into a city of alpinists come climbing season. Each year, alpinists died while making their way from Base Camp through the treacherous Ice Fall en route to the summit. It seemed a wild and fated place, a portal to peril and a desolate crossroads of adventure and ambition. I thought if I saw it with my own eyes, maybe I would finally stop thinking about the mountain and all those who'd been lost to it.

The trek we planned would take us on a loop through the Khumbu region south of Everest, a well-beaten route that climbs through villages, over 17,700-foot Cho La Pass, and then to Base Camp. We hired a Sherpa guide named Jangbu; his assistant, Rinche, who would be our cook; and several porters to carry our camping gear.

I turned thirty-one in Nepal. The night of my birthday, Rinche baked a pistachio cake, complete with candles. We were in Namche Bazaar, the last big village before Base Camp, a four- or five-day walk away. We camped outside of town, on a grassy spot with our first view of Everest. It was late October, and darkness came well before 6:00 p.m., when the sun fell behind the tall, spiky peaks and didn't creep back up again until nearly nine in the morning. Looking back, it seems we spent all our time on the trek, a frozen eternity, huddled in our sleeping bags in our tent. We lay down so long each night, we joked, we were getting bedsores.

Namche Bazaar was cosmopolitan in comparison to the other villages we passed through; internet cafes lined its dirt roads; prayer flags flapped from buildings. You could buy anything in Namche: counterfeit North Face jackets, used books, twenty minutes of dial-up internet, postcards to send home. Signs advertising goods and services hung from facades, hopeful, homemade emblems of commerce with odd syntax that always made Steve laugh. LADIES AND ZEN'S, read one above a women's and men's hair salon.

Rinche's cake was dry and chalky on account of the altitude, but its decorations showed a flair for the fabulous. He laid shelled pistachios in a ring around the edge of the frosting, which was the color of young mold, but had the crumbly texture of very old meringue. We sat on a table outside and admired the cake. Nepal was in the midst of a Maoist rebellion, and we'd debated canceling our trek.

In the end, we decided to take the risk. Now, as Steve and Jangbu sang "Happy Birthday," it seemed our worries had been for naught.

Rinche had brought a cook kit of small, mismatched aluminum bowls and tin coffee cups with crooked handles. That evening as we cut into the cake, I noticed a small label stuck to the side of one container. KEEP SUFFICIENT FOOD ACCORDING TO SIZE, it read.

I showed it to Steve. "What do you think *that* means?"

He shrugged and grinned. "Who the hell knows?" he said, biting into the dusty cake.

We laughed a lot on that trip. We laughed when we got to the top of Gokyo Ri at 18,000 feet and I discovered that Steve had hidden three softball-sized rocks in my backpack as a joke to slow me down. We laughed at the cows grazing alongside the runway in Kathmandu, and we laughed in terror at the runway in Lukla that sloped uphill. We laughed, but only in retrospect, after our three-wheeled *tuktuk* crashed into a car on the way to the airport to begin our trek, sending boxes of food spilling into the roadway and breaking all the eggs Rinche had bought for the trip.

We laughed so we didn't cry about having to sleep in the tent for a thousand frozen hours in a row, getting up in the middle of the night to make sure our legs still worked, and seeing the most brilliant light show of stars dazzle the sky above Ama Dablam. We laughed with mortification after throwing up Rinche's deep fried yak in a meadow all night long.

It would take months, but eventually we would be able to laugh at the fact that we didn't made it to Everest Base Camp after all. At 17,500 feet we were too weak to continue climbing, so we descended instead and spent the night outside the Tibetan Buddhist monastery of Tengboche before finally decamping to a beach in Thailand, where we gorged on Pad Thai and gained back the ten pounds we'd each lost in the mountains.

I took it as a promising sign that we could laugh even when we were so sick, so far from home, ravaged by altitude, darkness, and cold, lumbering downhill in a propeller plane, flying sideways through storm clouds with such abandon it seemed as though all the screws would pop loose.

—

Right effort becomes my running mantra. If I can train without striving for a specific result or worrying about how other runners train and whether I'm doing enough, I will be happier. And if I'm happier, unburdened by expectations and pressure, I'll run healthier. I'll be more likely to avoid injury and burnout. I might actually have a shot at finishing Leadville, which, if I'm being honest with myself, is my only objective.

I vow not to get hung up on details or data but to do what I love and what moves me, literally: walk the dog, coach our girls' lacrosse team, hike with Steve. Do I feel like riding my bike to the river after dinner in the fading light to sit with my bare feet in the cold water and meditate for five minutes? Yes, I do.

Do I want to hike Sun Mountain with Pippa at dawn to watch the lunar eclipse?

Yes.

Just like sitting, everything counts.

The problem is, running is so much lonelier than it used to be. After my father died, I could run for hours and never need to talk to anyone. I talked to myself, and to my father, I talked to the mountains and the memories swirling through my body, I talked to my body. I needed the silence and scale of wilderness to absorb my grief. Now, though, I no longer hunger for solitude. What I crave is connection.

I invite my friends to run with me. I go too far, too fast, they say, at weird times of day. They agree to join me for short stretches; a few miles here and there. I'll take anything I can get: through a sandy canyon to the river before work, around the town trails. At the sight of their faces, I am instantly, gloriously relieved.

One day in early March when the winter light is still weak, I go out alone after breakfast into the foothills. My muscles are sluggish, my mood low. After five or six miles, I find I can't take another step. It's not that my legs are tired or don't work. It's my heart. It's just too heavy. It weighs 3,000 pounds, but also it's so light it feels as though it could flap right out of my chest.

The realization fells me like a load of lumber: I simply cannot run home. I sit down, hugging my knees. I could call Steve to come and get me; I could walk home. I do neither. Instead I do the only thing I can think of, the one thing I've never done before while running: I lie back, spreadeagle on the ground, half in the middle of the trail, half off. If I can flatten myself to the earth, maybe I will be able to feel it spinning beneath me, pulling me into its force field. Maybe then I won't feel like I'm flying alone off the edge.

The ground is surprisingly soft and the pine needles push through my thin shirt, prickling my back in a bristly, satisfying way that reminds me I still have nerve endings, that I'm alive. I crack my eyes to look at the sky; it's a deep, show-offy blue, a shade so fake it makes you lift your sunglasses to see if it's real. It feels good to lie here, so uselessly, equal parts earth and air.

I spread my arms and legs wide like a starfish to feel the maximum amount of earth beneath my body. If someone were to come upon me, they might think I am dead or asleep, but I am neither. I am very much awake. Sprawled out in the dirt, I swear I can detect the earth's deep, resonant hum moving through me, supporting me. Then, slowly, after a long while, I roll over to one side, rise to my feet, brush the pine needles from my skin, and run home.

Running is a kind of alchemy: you put what's in your heart and mind into your running and it transforms into energy, a kind of wild release—some days, almost, but not quite, the next best thing to euphoria. For years, I'd shoveled my fear and grief into running and it came out as power, sometimes even joy. Now, though, no part of me wants to go out for miles by myself—an unexpected new development that I find minorly alarming.

In my notebook, I worry it into a story:

> *I'm no longer mentally tough.*
> *I used to be tougher.*

How easy it is to become attached to the way things once were, to how we used to behave, to our old proclivities and habits and identities, especially if they were successful or admired. But things always change. *We* always change. How much kinder we'd be to ourselves if we were curious about the changes, instead of resisting them, judging them.

An alternate story I could tell myself: *I'm creative, I solve problems. I know what I need.*

On a hunch, I start splitting my long runs in two: twenty miles in the morning, eight or ten in the late afternoon. In between, an icy shower and a big lunch. I've never done this before, assuming that at my age, after surgery, my body would balk at running twice a day.

In fact, the opposite is true. My legs are always sluggish at the start of the second run, but after a couple miles they perk up, cheerfully adapting to the exertion I ask of them. It's such a relief not to have to support myself for six hours alone—less committing, less exposed, not nearly so desolate.

One day I plot a route that takes me eighteen miles along the base of Atalaya and winds up at the girls' school for Maisy's second-grade end-of-year picnic. Her class is outside in the garden and one of the dads is grilling hamburgers on a barbecue. Trays of cookies line a table; I open a large cooler and find it full of Gatorade. The picnic is an aid station! I eat a burger and a brownie, gulp down a Gatorade, and sit for half an hour talking with Maisy and the other parents. When the teacher calls the children back to class, I put on my pack, hug Maisy goodbye, and keep running.

—

Buddhism was on display everywhere in Nepal. Steve and I passed *stupas*, temples hung with faded prayer flags. Wooden prayer wheels lined the entrance to small villages, built atop rock walls made from intricately carved prayer stones, called *mani* stones. You were supposed to spin the prayer wheels as you walked by while chanting the Buddhist mantra *Om Mani Padme Hum*—"the jewel is in the lotus"—under your breath, as Steve did, in a low, trance-like voice whenever we passed the chiseled rocks.

It was in one of these villages that I bought a used copy of *The Snow Leopard*, Peter Matthiessen's account of a trek he took through Nepal in 1973 with wildlife biologist George Schaller. The paperback was creased, its pages soft and water stained. I read it by headlamp each night in our tent, my sleeping bag pulled up to my chin. Matthiessen was a New Yorker with a serious Zen practice and a grief-stricken heart. I knew almost nothing about Buddhism or meditation then and read the book as an account of his two-month trek to study Himalayan blue sheep and perhaps spot an elusive snow leopard. Matthiessen's scientific observations bored me vaguely, but I liked that he was searching for something he was unlikely to find.

Years later, I pulled the same wrinkled copy from my bookshelf and opened to a page in the middle. The whole story came back to me: endless nights in a frozen tent, the smell of burning dung wafting from teahouse chimneys, long arduous ascents over mountain passes, stalking the rare leopard. It was now the middle of the pandemic, and I was restless and bored, grateful that Matthiessen's diary entries swept me off to a foreign land. This was how I remembered *The Snow Leopard*, as an expedition journal. When I reread it, though, I saw it was all Zen parts I'd underlined.

For years after our trek, Steve and I laughed about the label on Rinche's dish. KEEP SUFFICIENT FOOD ACCORDING TO SIZE became our inside joke, a one-liner whenever we had leftovers to reheat and a catchall for anything clumsily expressed, mystifying, or just plain weird. Deep down, though, I knew it meant something more than its mangled literal translation. It had morphed into an enigmatic Zen koan I could spend my whole life trying to understand.

Peter Matthiessen went to Mustang in hopes of seeing a snow leopard, but his quest was much more than a wildlife expedition. He was mourning his wife, who'd died of cancer the year before. He was on "a true pilgrimage, a journey of the heart," searching for a deeper understanding of Zen and impermanence.

I lay in bed rereading *The Snow Leopard*, mesmerized by it in a way I hadn't been in Nepal, devouring the Zen teachings Matthiessen doled out in brief, tantalizing increments. I was three-quarters of the way through the book—Matthiessen had set up camp in a cold courtyard in a deserted monastery at the base of Crystal Mountain, overlooking the Black River—when I was struck by a burning need to know.

I turned to Steve beside me in bed and gestured to the book. He'd read it too, all those years ago in Nepal. "Do you remember? Does he ever see a snow leopard?"

"Hmmm?" Steve asked idly, not looking up from his pages.

In the pause between my question and his response, I remembered that I knew the answer. The answer was no. Matthiessen did not see a snow leopard; the knowledge of this, a detail long dormant, rose in me. I turned the page. The author had been tracking the leopard's sign for days; if he didn't see it, it wasn't because the leopard had left. It was because Matthiessen wasn't ready to perceive it. He climbed to a small Tibetan Buddhist shrine, or *gompa*, notched into the side of Crystal Mountain. An elderly lama sat on a ledge, wordlessly whittling a stick. Matthiessen imagined the lama asking him, "Have you seen the snow leopard?"

And in his mind, Matthiessen answered, "No. Isn't that wonderful?"

—

Running one hundred miles means holding two seemingly contradictory ideas in my mind at the same time: include everything and keep sufficient food according to size. Do all I can to stay in motion, to stay inspired and curious, but don't put too much in the container. Run with right effort. This isn't license to be lazy or aimless. Matthiessen traveled vast distances on foot, making eight trips over Kang La Pass, hauling heavy loads, post-holing through snow up to his waist. This was, as Dogen would have described it, total exertion, an unending practice. But when Matthiessen finally arrived at Shey Monastery, even after expending such tremendous effort, he found he was not attached to the outcome after all.

Some days the paradox is a puzzle I will never solve, but out on the trails, moving swiftly and without thought, it is the truest thing I know about running and writing and being alive.

22. BEAST MODE

One morning in May, I wake up and know we are through it.

I don't know how I know this, I just do. Maybe it's the way the sun slants through the French doors in our bedroom, through the half-parted curtains we never close. There's more space in the room, or the space that is there is brighter, as though a clearing away has happened. Nothing has been said, but I can feel it. Steve rolls over and gets up first to make the coffee. I lie in bed staring at the wooden beams of the ceiling, sensing the change.

Something has burned off.

The anger.

It had been lodged inside of me, very deep, and now it has lifted.

The lilacs are blooming, my favorite time of year. Each morning I walk the girls to school and take the long way home, burying my face in every lilac bush I see. I feel it when I walk. I'm lighter. My friends told me I should forgive Steve, that it was an accident. I knew this, and I also knew that it would take the time it did, that it would come from inside me. I didn't know it would take so long or that I had been holding so much or that maybe my anger wasn't even about the accident; maybe it was older than the accident, older, even, than me.

Possibly the burning off had already happened, many months before, a slow accrual of affection and understanding that I can only feel now that it's over at last. There will be other things, surely. There always are. But this part is over.

—

Sometimes in the evenings, when I'm out walking, I fall in love with my shadow. It's after dinner, and the sun is low and caramel, and our dog Pete's shadow lopes beside me like a shaggy wolf. I walk fast, swinging my arms, happy and aware of my happiness.

The shadow-girl beside me is slim and fast. She has no doubts: her hips are loose and her stride long. Occasionally she shakes her hair as she moves. She is listening to music in her earbuds, loud. I can tell she wants to dance. She is young, no more than nine or ten, the age Pippa is now, still unselfconscious but not for long. I love my shadow, I want to be her, then realize that I am her.

When I go see my therapist, M, I try to explain how it is to walk with myself, free and happy, as the sun goes down. M is an artist of indeterminate age. He could be sixty or seventy-five; his hair is smooth and such a dark, glossy black I can pretend he is not old and will never die. I've been seeing him for so long I've lost count of the years. His impeccable, muted gray office never changes—the subdued black and white photographs of clouds, not one single thing ever out of place.

"I *am* young," I tell M, and from the adamance in my voice I can tell that I'm trying to convince myself, as much as him.

"You will always be young," he replies, and in that moment I love him very much.

—

I don't say anything to Steve about the change I feel between us. I'm afraid of trying to explain it and failing. I'm afraid of spoiling it, of him saying, "It's taken you *this* long?" Instead, I ask him if he wants to go for a run. We used to run together, years earlier, before I started racing and he started fly-fishing. I miss the easy way we talk when we are moving together along a trail, one of us in front, the other behind, in a place where we speak truthfully, at home with ourselves and each other, outside.

It's a Thursday evening, well after six when we leave the trailhead and begin running through the forest on a narrow trail beside a creek. We say little for a long while; climbing is an effort and I focus on my body and the resistance in my mind. I'm trying to decide if I'm going to sign up for a fifty-mile race to prepare my legs and lungs for Leadville. Races make for good training runs; every few miles there are aid stations stocked with food and chipper volunteers to goad you along. This race is in two days. I've been holding it loosely in my mind for the past month, waiting to see if I felt ready, so I don't put too much pressure on myself.

About three and a half miles in, Steve and I stop along the stream in a meadow to look for tiny darting trout slinking beneath rocks at the water's edge. The forest smells sweet yet dry, like summer in the Rocky Mountains: warm dirt and sunbaked pine needles.

It reminds me of Idaho.

"I want to go back to the Middle Fork again someday," I blurt. Saying it out loud feels spontaneous, as though it comes out of nowhere, but I know that's not true. It comes from the sweet scent of a summer forest and from the deepest, realest part of me, where there's no hesitation or fear.

We talk about it as we run, the terrible thing that had happened and how we wish it hadn't.

"There were so many problems with that trip, so many things that went wrong," Steve says.

"We shouldn't have launched in such a hurry without the older guys giving us the lay of the land, without a plan," I agree.

"I couldn't see the other boats in front of us. I should have pulled off that rock harder," he says. "It wasn't that I got pushed into it. Most every other boat did. It was that I waited too long for the raft to bounce off when I needed to have rowed off."

He's in front, I'm behind. I have to catch my breath. He's never said this before. "I wish you'd been able to run the trail like you wanted to."

For the first time since the accident, there's no blame, no recrimination, no bitterness, just a quiet, clear-eyed regret that feels almost like peace. Bounding downhill in the clear evening light, we've closed the door, let go. Nearly two years have passed. We've come through it together.

When I get home, I sign up for the fifty-mile race.

The next morning, I visit Natalie in her garden. "Just sit," she says, motioning to her plastic lawn chair. I always go see Natalie before a race. She knows the exact right thing to say to calm my nerves, and it's rarely about running. Her spring garden is lush, an explosion of roses and irises, like a painting.

A few days earlier, she'd taken Maisy to the Georgia O'Keeffe Museum downtown. Children need art, Natalie is forever telling me, in the same pointed tone she used to inform me that artists need to meditate. Natalie is a painter and has taken it upon herself to educate Maisy in the fine arts. After all, she's known Maisy since she was just a pair of chubby infant legs dangling out of my hiking pack when we first started walking up the mountain.

Nat is a good teacher. Every so often she comes over with armfuls of art books and she and Maisy turn the pages slowly, studying the works with great care, and then paint their own. At the museum, they sat together on the floor, studying one abstract in particular that they both admired. It was a painting of three lumpy green peaks backed by a bright red-orange glow that could have been the setting or the rising sun. Or maybe it was fire, or a burst of lightning turning the whole sky gold. It was all things all at once. It was called *Anything*.

From her perch in the garden, Natalie shakes her head, remembering the painting. "*Anything*," she whistles admiringly. "Can you believe that title? Doesn't it just kill you?"

It's true. "The whole word fits into *Anything*," I agree. "No good, no bad, everything."

After Maisy came home from the museum, she showed me the pastel she'd made, a swirl of peaches and blues that looked like a creamsicle in the ocean. It was so perfect I wanted to eat it. On the back, in her blocky, seven-year-old handwriting, she'd given it a title, the letters slanted but unmistakable: *Forgiven*.

When I tell Nat this now, she closes her eyes for a long time like it's too much to take in, because it is. It really is. These iridescent little sparks, lighting up out of nowhere.

—

The Jemez Mountains Fifty is a competitive ultramarathon that attracts top runners training for summer hundred-milers. Even if I stick to my plan of right effort—running for distance, not for the win—it will in no way be a sightseeing excursion. It's been two years since I've run this far. In April, my friend Ruthanne and I ran thirty-two miles from Santa Fe to the village of Chimayo as part of a traditional Easter pilgrimage. Chimayo is home to a 200-year-old *santuario* famous for its healing dirt that the devout claim returns the injured and ill to health. Thousands walk the pilgrimage route along highways and main roads to Chimayo every spring, but we took the long, back way, out a rutted dirt road nearly to the Rio Grande, along sandy trails and country roads, past barking dogs, farms, and craggy badlands all the way to Chimayo. When we got there, I scooped up a palmful of red dirt, patted it over the scar on my knee, and whispered a little wish for healing.

This is my favorite way to run long distances: in the company of a friend, in conversation and silence, in companionship and solitude, disconnected from time, yet connected—to each other and the land: it feels like traveling, not training. Races are different, of course, but I'd much rather race fifty miles in the company of others than run thirty miles by myself. I think about that morning on the trails when I couldn't run home. I hadn't been tired, I'd been lonely.

The race starts in less than twenty-four hours. It's time to go home and prep my gear. As I get up to leave, Natalie asks, "Do you know why running this far feels so scary?" I shake my head, knowing her answer will be different than mine. "Because it's the complete dissolution of the self."

I let her words wash over me. Yes. It sounds like the opposite of lonely. It sounds like running free.

"If you want to appreciate something fully, you should forget yourself," Suzuki Roshi wrote. "You should accept it, like lightning flashing in the utter darkness of the sky."

It's pitch black at the start, forty-five minutes west of Santa Fe, on the outskirts of Los Alamos. I've raced here twice before, winning the 50k race in 2012 (my first ultramarathon) and finishing second in the fifty-miler the following year.

Our feet kick up dust on the narrow trail that descends through a chute into a canyon. The rock is porous tuff, and clouds of white drift through our head lamp beams and into our eyes, sticking like grit to our teeth. I feel my pulse settle, finding a pace, holding to it. Up a long ridge, into sunrise. Everything is beautiful, more beautiful than I remember. We trace the path of a recent forest fire, through charred skeleton trees and young aspens sprouting chartreuse out of the blackened ground.

It's unexpected, then, when I feel panic rising like a lump in my throat. What if I can't finish? What if I fall down with my heart beating out of my chest? Who could I ask for help? I'm miles from an aid station. There are no other runners nearby.

"It's okay," I say aloud.

My voice startles me. I'm talking to myself, but it does not seem unnatural. It's comforting. "You're doing great. Everything's going to be alright."

I think about Steve and the girls at home and how I wish they were here to cheer for me. What would I want them to say to me? What would I need them to say?

"I'm proud of you."

I repeat it because saying it out loud makes me feel less scared, less lonely.

"I'm proud of you."

The trail twists up the burned mountainside, following gentle looping switchbacks. I keep my pace while talking aloud.

"I love you."

This is what I want them all to say. Steve, who always supports me but not always my running, my mother, who worries for me and doesn't understand why I run, and all the other voices inside and outside that suggest running is selfish, indulgent. This is what

I want them to say to me, but even more, it's what I need to say to myself. What we all need to say to ourselves.

"You are so strong."

"Just run."

I'm alone out here, but not really. I have myself. I can be my own champion.

"I am going to take care of you from now on."

—

Years ago, before babies and marriage, Steve and I took a road trip to Death Valley and the Eastern Sierra. It was the fourteenth of March when we pulled into Stovepipe Wells at ten feet above sea level, the nadir of North America—the last day of the tourist season before the motel would close for the summer. We ate dinner in the park cafeteria next to the campground, counter-service chicken fingers and cold, flabby French fries. The whole place had a shutting-down feel to it, marked most significantly by a steady stream of park employees and tourists heading for the exit. We had the sense of swimming against the tide, of the usual order of things not making sense.

At sunrise, we hiked out to the pink dunes. They were wild and steep, hundreds of feet tall, shifting hills of sand. We were the only ones there. On top, Steve squatted on the dune and scooped sand into his palm. It was less pink than a rich cream, very fine and pale, almost dust. A light breeze gave the illusion that we were swaying in midair, tethered neither to ground nor sky. In all directions, the desert blanketed the earth, bare and tan, a great many miles to the base of the mountains. Steve was transfixed by the rippled sand, but I couldn't stop staring at the horizon, the peaks of the Panamint Range and the Eastern Sierra rising in the distance. I was here but wanted to be there.

This feeling had dogged me for so long, maybe forever: being caught between two places and a multitude of emotions. I stood with Steve on the dunes and wanted not to feel this way any longer. Was this what making a life together meant? You could stand in the same place and really be there with each other, no longer pulled by far-off places, imaginary or real? I didn't know, but I wanted to find out.

All week, wherever we went, I found Steve bent over, studying the tiny, bright desert wildflowers, miniature denizens of almost unimaginable hardship. "Here, look at this," he'd say, rattling off Latin names, marveling at their delicate hardiness—such a baffling contradiction—while I squinted and tried to listen, to see those desert survivalists with the same awe: the way they grew out of a cleft in the rocks, out of cracks in the parched earth. It was dizzying to look down for so long. Perhaps Steve felt the same way looking up.

On the last day of our trip, we traipsed through pockets of knee-deep snow to a grove of ancient bristlecone pines on a high slope in the Eastern Sierra. Stout and gnarled, some nearly 4,000 years old, they were the oldest living specimens on the planet. They had been shaped by centuries of wind and weather and light and darkness, change so constant and yet so protracted it was hard to comprehend. It seemed impossible that something so still and so old could still be alive, still growing. And yet they were. You could feel them.

Steve and I walked side by side, running our hands along the bristlecone's pocked bark and limbs, too awed to speak. The quietude here was different than the sun-battered silence of the desert. It was the stillness not of retreat or withdrawal but of watchfulness, of trees standing sentry, shoulder to shoulder, attentive to the near and the far. This time, I could see it—the astonishing beauty up close, braided branches twisting with outstretched arms, reaching but at the same time curling back on themselves in a strange, intimate embrace.

—

The choking panic is gone and now I can just run. I can be the person I need for myself. All the long miles through the Jemez Mountains blur. I can't tell you what happened in which order, only that at each aid station I take slices of oranges and watermelon and cups of ginger ale. I am saying no to nothing today.

I stop at an aid station at mile forty-seven. It's hot now, the glaring midday sun blasting down on us, and a volunteer wrings ice water from a sponge onto my neck. A runner comes up behind me wearing what looks at first glance to be a Viking hat and a kilt. I must be hallucinating, but then through my earbuds I hear him yelling at me, "You're an animal! You're running such a strong race!" He flashes me a thumbs up and screams, "Beast mode!"

Even a few hours earlier, I might have dismissed him as insincere or myself as undeserving, but now I laugh and say, "Thank you," because I do feel strong. I *am* in beast mode.

It's been building in me all spring, and now I've run my way into it.

Suzuki Roshi had another name for beast mode. He called it big mind or universal mind, Zen mind. It's doing something completely, sincerely, and with an attitude of curiosity and composure— tapping into something inside and outside of ourselves that's bigger, more powerful than we could have ever imagined. It's knowing there is so much we don't know, may never know, and being open to whatever comes. "Cultivate your own spirit," he wrote. "It means not to go seeking for something outside yourself. This is a very important point, and it is the only way to practice Zen."

In the end, I win the race. I finish with feet full of blisters I never felt forming. Soon they will turn into callouses I'll peel off in great stiff slabs, exposing the shock of pink baby skin beneath, feet reborn and resigned to hard wear and long days, outer layers shedding themselves to make way for the new.

I had talked myself off the loneliest ledge of despair and stayed in each moment as it came, and with myself most of all. "Big mind is calm mind," Suzuki Roshi said. "Big mind is something to express, not something to figure out. It is something you have, not something to seek for." Like big mind, you can't chase beast mode or will yourself into it. It's not a fixed point or a final destination but a quality of being. You don't get there by chance or luck or by trying but rather by *not* trying. It's not about winning, but being.

Beast mode won't carry you the whole distance or last forever, and the way there is different every time. But you know it when you're in it. It's like falling in love: you can't have it always, but be very glad when you do.

PART FOUR

SKY

23. PHENOMENAL EXPRESSION

"For the time being, stand on top of the highest peak," Dogen wrote in "Uji," his famous essay about time. There comes a moment on almost every mountain when you climb out of the forest, above all the trees. The air is thinner, clearer, the views longer. You can see every which way, in all directions—bowls and cirques, high ridges, mountains beyond mountains. You are in the air, almost flying.

The climb has been taxing, but here at the edge of the sky, the mountain gives you all its energy, fills you with a kind of exhilaration you rarely feel down low, in the trees.

Here you are closer to the sky. You are sky.

—

I don't want to tell this part of the story because it will mean it's over, but of course it *has* been over. It ended and the next thing began. "It's complete," M, my therapist, told me recently. The way he said it, with such finality, saddened me. I wanted to protest, *No, it keeps going. I know it does.* But I also knew that he was right, that both are true.

On the first day of summer, I leave for a three-day running camp in Leadville to prepare for the race. This will be my last big push, sixty miles over three days at high altitude on the same trails I will run in August. My body is ready, but my heart isn't.

It's June 23, two years to the day since I fell.

Two years patching together what we'd had, reassembling bones and hearts, two years since the rock split the river, my leg, and my life. Two years mending fractures small and large, beginning again.

I think back to the day we drove to Idaho, the apprehension I felt as our loaded truck bumped down the driveway. That morning, like this one, was a hinge point in a larger narrative that's still unfolding. It would be so much easier to stay home now, but then I wouldn't find out what happens next.

I count rivers on the drive north to take my mind off leaving. Some are so small you'll miss them if you don't know to look: the Rio Tesuque, the Santa Cruz. Others, like the Rio Grande and Rio Chama, are wide and brown and slow. The last watershed before Leadville is the Arkansas River, a torrent of whitewater draining the 14,000-foot peaks of the Sawatch Range. You know you're almost there when the river, six rafts wide when you first saw it, winnows to a creek you can nearly jump across.

The two-bedroom Victorian I've rented in Leadville has purple gingerbread trim and a folksy sign in the kitchen that reads TODAY IS A GOOD DAY. I decide to go with that. When I peer through the front curtains, though, all the houses on Second Street are dark. I miss Steve and the girls. I know no one in town. Not a soul.

It had seemed like such a good idea! All of it—healing myself and running one hundred miles and coming here to train on the course. But now it's midnight and my heart is panic-whomping in my chest as I lie in bed counting my breaths, willing myself to stay alive.

Finally, dawn. A cold, sharp morning at 10,000 feet above sea level, even on the longest day of the year. A skim of frost prickles the grass in the weedy backyard. It's thirty-eight degrees when I put on my down jacket and ride my bicycle up the street for the first group run, twenty-six miles from Turquoise Lake to the village of Twin Lakes—a full marathon, but still only a quarter of the race. I try not to think about this while I run. The air is cool and fresh, and we climb steadily along the Colorado Trail toward the summit of Sugarloaf Mountain. It's easy to keep an even pace and not feel taxed, to feel happy and realize that I am happy.

Yet I can't relax. I keep checking my watch to see how much time has passed, trying to guess my pace and calculate how far I've run, five miles by now, or seven? I'm not in a rush, but I feel as though I'm pushing something—my ego, maybe. Pride. I want to run fast and finish well, even though I'm not racing any of the runners behind me, only myself. Only the clock.

When I finally arrive at the town hall in Twin Lakes, five or six guys who've come in before me are stretching their tan, lanky limbs across picnic tables like rubber bands. They shoot me quizzical looks, as though they're surprised to see a woman in their midst, as though it's possible I'd ducked into a later part of the trail and run only part way. After a while, a guy in an orange down jacket walks up to me and asks what everyone else is thinking, "Did you run here from Turquoise Lake?" His accent is smooth and southern, like a country singer, and he has friendly eyes.

"Yes," I answer, smiling back. I'm not offended. It doesn't matter what he thinks. I know what I did. I ran all the way here from Turquoise Lake and in six weeks I'm going to do it again.

I wake the next day determined to make a different plan for the second training run. I'm not going to push against time or the mountains. It wasn't very fun, it felt like work, tight and small with wanting. I sit in the darkened living room for ten minutes, meditating. A thought floats up on my breath, rising through my belly: the mountains have energy. I can fight them, or I can run with them.

I climb on my bicycle and ride up the hill. It's cold again, and my legs are tired but not sore, and pedaling on such a bright morning makes me glad. Riotous orange California poppies push through chain-link fences, growing frantically, unapologetically. There are maybe thirty nights a year without frost in Leadville, and this was one of them. We are going to run twenty-two miles from Twin Lakes up and over 12,600-foot Hope Pass and back.

Leaving Twin Lakes, the trail to the top of the pass becomes steep almost right away, and I alternate between jogging and hiking, catching up to a few men and using them methodically, one after another, to work my way six miles up the mountain. Gradually it dawns on me that I'm doing it: I am riding the mountain's energy to the top, just like I'll ride it all the way down.

We turn around at the abandoned mining town of Winfield and retrace our route, just as we will on race day. My second time up

Hope Pass from the other direction is easier because I know what's coming. I'm making a relationship with the mountain. A guy with a green shirt and a handlebar mustache is in front of me, and I use him, too, propelling myself uphill as though we're connected by an invisible tether, until eventually I pass him and roll over the saddle and all the way down the other side. Afterward, at the pop-up tent at the finish, where volunteers are grilling burgers, he comes over to me, smiling, and asks, "So where's your motor?"

I answer without thinking, "In the river beneath my feet."

He looks at me strangely and smiles, the smile you give someone when you think they might be a little nuts.

But I know what I meant, in my body. Beneath my shoes was solid ground, but the mountains are fluid, alive. They have a flow, an energy older and wiser that can carry me, the way rivers have always carried me. Even on the day on the Middle Fork when I broke my leg. There's a current, and you can fight it or go with it. I'd felt it that day in California, when I'd run like the river falling out of the sky.

Now I know the feeling I want to run with on race day. I've put it into my body. All I have to do is hold it in my mind.

—

Later, at the house on Second Street, I drag a plastic lawn chair onto the shaggy lawn beside the peeling picket fence. A clothesline sags above me. Gray clouds slide by, felt-bottomed. I have a book and a bar of chocolate and am content to sit here all afternoon, reading and writing and watching the sky.

When I look up, a woman is riding by on a bicycle with upright handlebars. She might be seventy. She pedals slowly but deliberately, her back straight as an arrow, her eyes forward. I go back to my book. A few moments later, she pedals back the other way. Her red windbreaker flaps in the breeze. Back and forth she rides, with such consistency, so little variation, not once looking left or right, it could almost be performance art. There are hundreds of streets in Leadville, but this must be the one she rides on Saturday afternoons.

The sky is blue turning to gray, weather moving in from the west. Something cracks the clouds—but it's not rain, it's light. The woman's steadiness is so dazzling I can't look away. "Every existence is a flashing into the vast phenomenal world," Suzuki Roshi wrote.

I sit watching her go back and forth for a long time, mesmerized, feeling as I did that day by the lake, watching the sailboat after my Uncle Phil's memorial, or climbing the mountain at home that's not mine but is the one I know and love best.

There's no group run on the schedule until the next evening, so in the morning I go looking for a mountain. To the east of Leadville, the peaks are all piled up together in the way mountains appear consolidated from afar, but when you get closer, you see they are distinct from each other, separated and connected by ridge lines and saddles. They are one and also not one.

The mountain I'm looking for is 14,000-foot Mount Sherman. I leave without a map and walk up a peak that two hikers say is Sherman, but when I climb up a steep drainage and across soft patches of old snow to the top, I'm greeted by a sign: DYER MOUNTAIN, 13,855 FT.

I'm with Tim, the runner with the twangy drawl, and we howl with laughter at our mistake and glissade down the snowfields nearly to the bottom and get back into Tim's borrowed old Land Cruiser and keep looking for Sherman. We are just going to find the trailhead for next time, we agree, but as we bump up the lopsided dirt track, I can tell we're doing more than scouting the route. I know that we will keep going until we find the trailhead, and even though it's after 5:00 p.m. and we have to be back in time for dinner before our night run, we will decide to go for the summit.

200 feet below the top, a screaming wind nearly shears me off the knife-edge ridge. I shelter behind a rock while Tim forges ahead. For once, I don't need to go farther. I am content to stop short. I've already found what I came for: a long, happy day in the mountains that I can put into the bank of my body so that I will

always remember the mountain's energy and my own true effort, the thin air and the salty tears that streamed down my face in the wind as I laughed.

We run all the way down, legs and arms flying, skidding wildly through ankle-deep scree, and still we miss dinner.

—

Our last run is fifteen miles from Turquoise Lake back to the finish line in Leadville. When I tally the miles I've covered in the last three days, it is nearly eighty-five, some of it unplanned, spontaneous, possibly ill-advised. And yet eighty-five miles will be the precise distance I will have run on race day by the time I reach Turquoise Lake. By some stroke of serendipity or hapless good luck, I've managed to mimic race conditions almost exactly.

The mountains have energy, I think as I run along the water's edge. It's nearly dark, a fat, sinking moon casting white ripples across the lake. Tim is on my heels, and by the time we reach the outskirts of town, it's after ten and the moon has set. We stop for a moment to turn off our headlamps and look at the stars, a zillion unknown galaxies blinking back at us. We've been talking for miles but now we're quiet, each of us trying to imprint the night into our bodies and minds so we can find our way back here in six weeks.

Leadville gleams out of the darkness. On the final half-mile along Harrison Avenue, the lights are off in all the houses, but I narrate the home stretch like it's race night. "Here they are, folks!" I shout into the empty sky. "They're coming into the final stretch! It's Tim from Kentucky! He's making it look easy!" I cup my hands to my mouth, imitating the hushed roar of the crowd as we hurtle down the last slope into town to where the finish line will be. "Here she comes, Katie from Santa Fe! Look at their blistering pace, folks, can you believe it?! They said it couldn't be doooonne!"

—

There's a saying in Zen: before enlightenment, chop wood, carry water; after enlightenment, chop wood, carry water.

After Leadville, the laundry.

I miss the mountains and the cool mornings, the brilliant orange poppies and the pastel-painted Victorians crowded together along narrow streets, but the mountains most of all. I'm trying to make sense of what happened. What *had* happened? I'd fallen in love—with Leadville and the trails, the community of runners who'd arrived as strangers, but many of whom were leaving as friends, with the leaning picket fences and the white dandelion fluff blowing through the air beneath the clothesline without pegs, the clouds striding by overhead, and with myself. All of it. Reading and writing and being glad and alive, not lonely, but full. I'd found my own wildness again.

Now, though, there are the girls' birthday parties to plan, and runs to be done before the house wakes up, and the wild, beautiful hum of home. "Zazen practice and everyday activity are one thing," Suzuki Roshi wrote. "Usually we think, 'Now zazen is over, and we will go about our everyday activity.' But this is not the right understanding. They are the same thing. We have nowhere to escape. So in activity there should be calmness, and in calmness there should be activity. Calmness and activity are not different."

Years earlier, when Pippa and Maisy were very small and I was strung out on fatigue and grief and trying to find a few minutes here and there to meditate, my therapist, M, suggested I meditate while they were in the bath. In the *bath*? I asked incredulously. Had he ever raised babies?! Was there anything less conducive to calmness than trying to bathe two squirming, slippery naked toddlers? I said as much.

"Meditation isn't precious, you just do it right in the middle of life," M replied. I knew so little about M—he had fantastic, fortress-like boundaries—but he'd dropped enough clues over the years that I knew he was a student of Zen, too.

One night I tried it. I sat there as the girls sloshed and slid around the tub, counting my breath, in and out. Two minutes at most. It was insane. It worked.

There is no difference between Zen and real life, writing and real life, running and real life—everything is all mixed up together, all at once.

A few days after I get home from Leadville, I listen to a podcast from the Zen center in town. It's about one of Dogen's best-known essays, called "Mountains and Waters Sutra," but I've not heard of it before. The young teacher recites its opening lines: "Mountains and waters right now are the actualization of the ancient Buddha Way. Each, abiding in its phenomenal expression, realizes completeness. Because mountains are high and broad, the way of riding the clouds is always reached in the mountains; the inconceivable power of soaring in the wind comes freely from the mountains."

Dogen's words, written 800 years ago in China, chop me off at the knees. I *knew* it! Mountains *do* walk! They flow. I'd felt it with my whole being on Hope Pass, my legs absorbing energy from the earth, my torso bending to the slope of the hill, the slope showing me how to run on water beneath my feet, my body flowing uphill the whole way. The energy wasn't mine, it was bigger than me. It was all around, limitless.

In Zen, phenomenal doesn't mean exceptional. It's not a grand performance. It means ordinary: the tangible, physical realities right in front of us. The mountains and wind, the sun, our bodies moving through space, the black dog lying at our feet, a girl riding home on her bicycle beneath a sapphire sky. Each thing complete as it is, singular, needing nothing extra.

24. FOURTEEN

On the first of July, I'm on a plane to Canada. The girls and I are going to spend the month with my mother on the island in Ontario where she'd grown up, and where I have spent every summer of my life and now my daughters, too. Pippa and Maisy sit beside me on the airplane. When the flight attendant comes down the aisle taking drink orders, they ask for ginger ale. I turn to look out the window. We are following the jagged spine of the Rockies north. Below us are crenellated peaks, high alpine bowls and passes still pocked with snow, mountainous flanks fanning out like tree roots, holding fast to the earth.

Far below the plane, rivers cut like veins across the desert, branching and forking, splitting, brown and craggy and motionless from such great heights. Cotton ball clouds cast puffy shadows across the Nebraska plains, which soon give way to a precise grid of farms, everything at right angles, so tidy and blank from the sky, so full of order and possibility.

Any story could be written from here.

—

I was a student of Dogen now. Before I left Santa Fe, I bought a book of his translated essays, including "Mountains and Waters Sutra." Dogen's writings were even more obscure than Suzuki Roshi's, but I could see in his teachings the roots of *Zen Mind*, and I got them in the same weird, separated-at-birth kind of way.

When I told Natalie I was reading Dogen, she laughed and said, "Ohhh boy, you're in deep." But she could tell I was serious, that I felt for him and his teachings a true affinity. She started calling him my boyfriend. "As your boyfriend says...." she chuckled, whenever I mentioned him. She forwarded emails from the Zen center, writing, "There's a retreat next month on your boyfriend's teachings." I began to think of Dogen with a kind of tender possessiveness and fantasized that the kinship I felt was reciprocal and miraculous, spanning vast time and space. We belonged to each other, Dogen and I.

Some mornings before I meditated, I read from Dogen's classic essays, fascicles about time and practice, birth and death. They were so dense I could only absorb a page or two at a time. I appeared composed on my ratty cushion, but on the inside I was wild with understanding, as if I were reading my own mind.

"You know things other people don't," Natalie sometimes said to me, "but you don't know what you know."

I knew what she meant and I also knew nothing.

Dogen, like Suzuki Roshi after him, believed awakening wasn't a straight line or a ladder with steps you tick off in neat succession, first this, then that, until at last it happens and you're done. Enlightenment isn't a single destination or a static state. It's in us all the time, unfolding circuitously, revealing itself suddenly, in glimmers, when you least expect it.

"When you believe in your way, enlightenment is there," Suzuki Roshi wrote. Whether or not you are watching the sky, the sky is watching the sky. Darkness is always part of the process.

—

At the lake, I ran every day, driving my old wooden boat to trails on the mainland, and when I got home, I made a sandwich and lay on my back on the dock, looking at the sky. It was different above the water than above the mountains. Rather than puffing upward in tall, steepled peaks, the clouds were flat-bottomed, as though planed by an invisible sheath. They drifted so slowly and uniformly they appeared to be painted on, a ceiling adorned with a fresco of clouds, yet the ceiling wasn't static, it was moving, slowly but surely, like a paper reel, a paper sky. The clouds slid along as a unit, the uniform spaces between the flat bottoms staying more or less the same.

The waves gulped at the dock, sucked themselves under and rattled the boards beneath me. The lake's mood dictated our days.

Sometimes the water was frothy with whitecaps, other times flat and calm. It was always harder than I remembered to shift into the water's rhythm from the arid air of the high desert. I missed the mountains, climbing up them, applying myself to their slopes, pushing against them until I learned to move with them.

I was hungry all the time that summer. I ate mint chocolate chip ice cream every night and slept like a teenager, as though drugged, dreaming of boys I used to know when I was young. They wrote me letters that arrived by boat twice a week. In the drawer beside my bed was a manila envelope fattened by letters I hadn't looked at in decades. The boys came to me while I slept and when I woke I carried with me the strange sensation of being fourteen again, not quite a girl, not yet a woman, with sun streaks in my hair and pine sap on the soles of my feet.

After I put the girls to bed each night, I paddled around our island. My kayak was long and green, dented from years of being dragged across the dock. It was Ontario in early July, and it stayed light until after ten. I loved the lake at dusk. The water was quiet and still, the dark pine shoreline punctuated by the warm glow of cottages. Through the windows and screened porches I could see silhouettes flashing, lives briefly illuminated.

Our island was a mile and a half around. It took twenty-five minutes to circumnavigate it. I had known its shoreline my whole life, longer than any place I'd ever lived, more intimately, even, than Atalaya. The girl I'd once been—who'd gone away so long ago—had been coming home this whole time, after all.

Overhead the moon was half full, and to the east, Mars was rising above the trees on the far shore, gleaming orange like the tiny, faraway tip of a matchstick. Across the water, Venus hung bright white over the western shore. Venus was sinking and Mars was climbing, but for a moment they appeared exactly equidistant above the lake, eye to eye, as though winking at each other from a great distance, greeting each other across millions of miles and millennia. Together, they made a strange, beautiful symmetry. It was a rare conjunction, like lovers who would never meet, only admire each other from afar forever. *Hello, it's me.* It made my head swim just thinking about it.

A few days later I went looking for my mother in the kitchen. I was going on my last long run before Leadville and planned to be gone a few hours. The girls were out at sailing lessons, but I figured I ought to tell someone where I was going and when I would be home. She was cleaning up from breakfast and had her back to me, rummaging through the pantry.

"Hey, Mom," I said. "I'm heading out for a while to go running."

"Hmmm," she answered aimlessly, poking her head out of the closet. It was hard to tell when she was listening and when she was thinking about what to make for dinner, or if the weather and wind were favorable for hanging her freshly laundered sheets on the clothesline.

"I'll probably be gone about three hours." I always lowballed Mom because I knew my running worried her. She was afraid I was going to ruin my knees. I'd finally learned that it was pointless to try to convince her otherwise. It was better to tell her only what she absolutely needed to know, and even then, to round down.

She spun her head around to look at me. "How far are you going?" she asked.

"Oh, maybe twenty miles." My plan was at least twenty-three.

Mom groaned and wrinkled her face with exasperation, as if she had just eaten something sour.

My stepfather had come into the room. "Why do you do this?" he asked.

"I'm training," I said, my face reddening. I knew how they felt about my running: that it was excessive, self-involved, injurious. I had daughters and a husband to look after. I should not spend so much of my life running and writing private things that should stay secret. I should be more helpful. I had internalized this message for so long that it was difficult to distinguish their voices in my head from my own; maybe, unwittingly, part of me believed it, too.

Why, at forty-six years old, did I still feel as though I needed my parents' approval to run, and worse, why did I want it? I felt like yelling, but instead I just said, "See you later" and pushed open the screen door, letting it slam behind me.

—

There are certain ages that, when we look back on them, represent the essential, defining core of our character. Everyone's inner age is different; mine had always been seven. I was scrappy, with skinned knees, always getting into little dustups on my bike or falling out of trees. My mother joked that she didn't think I'd make it to ten. I guess I lived all-out, in the way that most seven-year-olds did in the 1970s, without worrying about dying or what other people thought or the climate crisis or social media, mass shootings, or pandemics. Life wasn't idyllic: there were high expectations and hours of boring chores and emotional land-mines scattered all over the house, but there was a baseline happiness to being seven.

Sometimes when I caught a glimpse of myself in the mirror, I was surprised to find that I was so old, when on the inside I was obviously seven.

Now I was fourteen again. Maybe it worked like that, time leaping forward and back in intervals, just like Dogen said: "Time moves from present to past." Fourteen was the summer between junior high and high school. Short shorts, no makeup, barely developed breasts. The summer I dreamed of boys but had no experience, might have been kissed once or twice, but was not yet saddled with obligation to the opposite sex or their expectations of me. Fourteen was maybe the very last year I felt truly free. My stepsister, Amy, and I played tennis until dark every night on sun-cooked courts that smelled of burned rubber. Tennis ball fuzz sprayed off our strings, our shots skimmed hard down the line, cross-courts barely clearing the net, until we lost the ball to the inky night sliding down from the sky.

—

When I got home, my stepfather was sweeping pine needles off the rock by the boat house steps, so slowly and deliberately and with so much precision, even more so than usual, that I knew he'd been waiting for me. The broom made a soft whisking sound as it brushed the rock, and he turned the bristles so that they nestled into the crevices where the pine needles bunched after a wind or a rain. I tied my boat and walked up the steps, bracing myself.

"Why do you do this?" he asked without looking up. The whisking had turned into an aggressive swatting. "It's a compulsion, an addiction."

"I'm training for a hundred-mile race next month. I'm a good role model for the girls," I answered.

"Role model for what? Running for four hours?"

"For having a dream," I retorted, "for setting goals, and going after them. Self-discipline." I paused. These were values I'd learned from him.

I remembered a word I'd heard the octogenarian runner and writer Bernd Heinrich use to describe his running: devotion. It sounded mystical, spiritual. True. I felt the word on my tongue but didn't say it out loud.

"You need to be more helpful," he said. He'd stopped sweeping and fixed his piercing, light-blue eyes on me.

I knew he was talking about all the times I lay on the dock with my notebook shading my eyes, listening to the water slosh against the wood. It did look as though I was doing nothing, but I was doing something, I was dreaming stories into being. The more he disapproved of my dreaminess, the dreamier I became. Sometimes when big boats plowed past, water from their wakes splashed up through the planks, leaving drops of smeared ink on my notebook paper, and my stepfather stalked by and I lay there, feeling lonely and defiant at the same time.

I turned to face him.

"I know you don't understand what I do," I said. "But I work. I write. I've written a book." I took a deep breath. I understood that we were saying things to each other that we'd thought for years, possibly forever, things that I wished I could say to Steve, too, and that I was culpable of not speaking up sooner, but I was saying them now, and it felt good, strangely thrilling and also frightening.

Then, spontaneously, I said something else:

"You know, I have a shot at this hundred-mile race. I could win it, and if I do, I might get sponsors, and if I get sponsors, I'll have a better chance of getting the word out about my book. And this would be good for my family."

I'd never once thought this, imagined or spoken it, not even inside my own head. Where had it even come from? I hadn't done a scrap of research. I didn't know who else would be racing Leadville, what the winning times had been, or even how fast I'd been running lately. But all those months and miles, it must have been growing inside me, and now that I'd said it, it sounded like it could almost maybe possibly be true.

I heard laughter, sharp as a slap. He turned to go, the broom dangling limply from one hand. He was done, with the sweeping and, I supposed, with me. I loved him even when I hated him, and I wanted him to love me. He was the only father I had left. I watched him leave, saying nothing.

That night I went out paddling much later than usual. Mars skimmed the trees, but across the lake Venus kept her distance, high in the sky, hanging out with the moon. Maybe she'd had it too, with waiting, with hoping to be seen and understood.

I was still fourteen even though I was also forty-six, and it did not seem unusual to be a teenager again at the same time I was a grown woman with two children to care for. I could be their mother and the girl with the rope bracelet fraying around my wrist, who drank Grape Crush through a licorice straw at the movie on Friday nights, hoping my fingers might graze those of the boy next to me. That summer before I fell in love, I did not cause trouble and came home when I was told, I listened to Bryan Adams on cassette, flipped the tape when it clicked to a stop, and pressed play again. Over and over. I knew I was different from my stepsister and other girls my age and was glad for it. I was making things on the inside, waiting for my moment, but I wasn't in any rush. It could take months or years. I did not realize it could also take decades.

Sometimes when I watched Pippa and Maisy at the lake, flinging themselves off the dock or running barefoot across the rocks, I felt wistful that it was their only summer being ten and eight. But maybe it didn't have to work that way.

One last morning, one last run, slow and sluggish on tired legs. Coming home across the lake, the water was calm, a deep indigo, almost oceanic. Leaving made me melancholy, but leaving had always been part of the arrangement. Coming to the island meant leaving the island, they were the same thing. You can't stop time, the best you can do is move with it, ride its slipstream like the waves rustling north on a gentle breeze.

—

July was over and we were going home to Santa Fe. It was the month I would run one hundred miles. Through the plane window flying south, I watched thick gray clouds convulse upward from a storm. Already I missed the lake, missed swirling my paddle through the soft black water after dark, feeling my way barefoot across granite ribbed with pearly seams, sneaking up the boathouse stairs after dark like I had when I was fourteen.

Some other day, I would be another multiple, forty-nine, and I would also be fourteen and seven and twenty-one and all the ages I ever was and will become. The world spins and we are full of love and joy and confusion and fear all at the same time. Babies get sick and people die and we cry and run many miles and push ourselves farther than we thought possible and still the grass grows and there are zucchinis in the garden and at the grocery store you can never remember whether to buy salted or unsalted butter.

25. ORDINARY

"Zen is not something to get excited about," Suzuki Roshi wrote in *Zen Mind Beginner's Mind*. In my crinkled copy of the book, I've underlined this passage twice, in different colored ink. Steve is good at being laid back, but not me. I tend to get excited, invested. I make up stories in my head and believe them. The stories are seductive, energizing. Only occasionally are they real.

"Our unexciting way of practice may appear to be very negative. This is not so. It is a wise and effective way to work on ourselves," Suzuki Roshi went on. "Just continue in your calm, ordinary practice, and your character will be built up."

But how can we live this way, really? We are humans with wild, erratic hearts full of longing and want. We fall in love and crave love. We love the idea of ourselves almost as much, and sometimes more, than we love other people. We collect so much stuff. We make mistakes and live in delusion, fool ourselves and others, tell the same stories over and over until we believe them. We have babies who clutch at us and to whom we clutch even more fiercely, with so much joy it nearly suffocates us. We cannot, will not, live without them. We are dazzled by success, seduced by significance; we fight and make up, cling by our fingernails to what we have and what we're terrified of losing. To be alive is to be attached.

The answer isn't to be apathetic, but to put care into your life as it is right now, not as it someday might be. Like the woman in Leadville on her bicycle: complete effort without concern for flashy results. "Zen is not some kind of excitement," Suzuki continued, "but concentration on our usual everyday routine." Each time you find yourself distracted or entranced by hypothetical scenarios, all you have to do is do the next real thing right in front of you.

Now I dreamed of Leadville. In one dream, I was at the running camp, but I'd misplaced my hydration bottles. I came into an aid station and couldn't find them. I looked all over and even went to a store to try to buy some, but no luck. All the while, other runners were passing me.

This dream did not make me anxious, only more determined. I knew how to take care of myself, and I would. In between the doubting me and the fierce, defiant me was the fourteen-year-old girl who was still so free she had nothing to prove.

Could I run one hundred miles as her?

—

I go to visit Natalie. I haven't seen her in six weeks, since before we left for Canada, and when I walk into her house, she exclaims, "Oh, Katie, you're older! You've grown!"

I feel my face flush, suddenly self-conscious. Has my summer tan made the wrinkles around my eyes more noticeable? It's quintessential Natalie to say the first thing that pops into her head, without filter, even if it is so honest it comes off as a little bit unkind. I feel so young and strong! Just last week I'd been fourteen! What can she see in me that I don't?

She studies me through narrowing eyes. "You've gotten taller." She gives a small nod, as though confirming something private for herself, pulls her hat from the coat tree, and motions for us to leave. We are going up the mountain, like we always do.

"What do you mean I look different?" I ask, following Natalie outside. I wonder if she can see the last month on my face, and if so, if I will tell her everything, and I know that I probably will.

She beams. "You look like a teenager."

—

"The more you understand your thinking, the more you find it difficult to talk about it," Suzuki Roshi had written. "The best way is just to practice without saying anything." I kept my Zen a secret from Steve, I didn't tell him I tried to meditate every day or that

I read *Zen Mind* like a bible or that I had a new boyfriend named Dogen or that I thought maybe I might actually be getting it, not in my brain but in my body, and that he might get it, too. No, I definitely did not do that. Zen wasn't a silver bullet, a hack. It was difficult sometimes, a lot of the time, to understand. Maybe it wasn't the answer at all but just one perspective. Of course this was true.

I slept a lot that week before Leadville, and I sat. What appeared like indolence was in fact preparation—but I didn't tell Steve this, either. He tends to become aggrieved before my big races, anticipating the toll they will take on both of us. Can I think of this as fear on his part, in the way that I tend to become anxious before a race? Perhaps it was the same emotion expressing itself differently: fear that was really love but was also fear. Of being left and lost, alone.

I tried to think of it that way.

A few months earlier, I'd asked Steve to pace me at Leadville. Runners are allowed to have someone run with them from the halfway point on, back to Leadville. Steve had kept me company at several races in the past, and his trademark mix of dumb dad jokes, laughter, and freakish composure had gotten me through many low patches. At Leadville he agreed to join me for twelve miles, starting at mile fifty. I assured him it would be mostly power hiking uphill—his forte—followed by a six-mile runnable descent, but he hadn't been running much, and I could tell he was worried about keeping up.

On Saturday before the race, Steve and I drove up to the peaks above Santa Fe for a trial run. It was too late to call it training, and anyway, Steve always out-hiked me easily on the climbs. We trekked fast up the trail to the bald summit of Deception Peak at 12,200 feet, bent over into the slope, talking the whole time. It was always easier for us up high, above the trees, free from all the ways we thought we had to be down low.

I'd been away for a month, and there was so much to catch up on. I told Steve about the course and what to expect: we'd run along the base of Hope Pass for a few miles before climbing steeply to the summit; I would need him to please remind me to eat an energy gel every thirty minutes so I didn't bonk. Shyly I got up my nerve to recount what I'd spontaneously told my stepfather that day at the lake—and what Pippa had surprised me by declaring, unprompted, the other day in the car, "Mama, I think you're going to win!" I didn't want to become attached to that outcome, and I certainly didn't want to talk about it, but I did want Steve to know I was trying to help support our family. This time, Steve's laconic response was exactly what I needed: he raised his eyebrows and nodded, a bemused expression on his face, and then he changed the subject.

We were talking about logistics, but really we were talking about love. By the time we got to the top, I was sure I could rely on Steve completely. But I already knew that.

How many times had we stood on top of Deception, gasping at the view? I'd memorized it by heart, but it was still magnificent: steep, rocky chutes funneling into an alpine lake; ravens circling the luminous sky; and far below, where the mountains gave way to crumpled up badlands, our house and girls, waiting.

—

For the first time before a race, I'm not anxious. I feel different in a way I can't completely pinpoint. Clearer, lighter. Ready.

That day at the lake, after I walked away from my stepfather walking away from me, I went into the boathouse. Maisy was there. She'd heard our whole exchange through the screen door. "It's okay, Mama," she said, hugging me. "I think you're doing a good thing. Don't worry."

Later that night, I taped the Leadville course map to the wall and pulled the race guide from a stack of papers I'd brought from Santa Fe. I studied the route, much of which I'd run in June, and reviewed the distance between aid stations, calculating how long it would take me to run from one to the next. I padded my time, rounding up to be safe. I typed these estimates into a spreadsheet, along with how many calories and what kind of fuel I would need to eat between and at each aid station. I calculated that if I was having a good day without major mishaps, I would finish in twenty-one to twenty-two hours.

I closed my laptop. Then I opened it again. I googled "winning women's times" at Leadville and scanned the results page. In the thirty-six-year history of the Leadville Trail 100, there had been many years when twenty-one hours was the winning female time.

My heart skipped a beat. I shut my computer and didn't think about it, but I didn't not think about it either. I looked at the map on the wall and thought about everyone who was going to help me, who believed in me, and that it was good, even when it was hard, to ask for help, and to do my best to help myself.

—

When Natalie and I get down from the mountain, I drive her back to her house. "Are you hungry?" she asks, then answers her own question without waiting for my reply. "You look hungry." She beckons for me to come inside. I sit at her kitchen counter while she fixes us eggs, as she often does after we walk.

"You know, you seem as good about this race as I've ever seen you," she says. "Better than you've ever been, actually. You seem so ordinary about it."

I laugh halfheartedly and wave my hand, feigning nonchalance. "Oh yeah, I'm just going to run a hundred miles next week, no big deal."

But she's not joking. "Your body is ready. Your body knows what do. Trust that and get out of your own way."

Driving home, I think about what she said. I know it's high praise, in Zen, but more than that, I know it's true. I do feel ordinary. I'm living the moments as they come, making green tea while thunder rumbles over the peaks, eating eggs with Natalie in her kitchen, going up and down, and down and up, the mountain.

"It is just very plain," Suzuki Roshi wrote, "When your practice is calm and ordinary, everyday life itself is enlightenment."

26. RUNNING FREE

It was so beautiful. It had all been so beautiful.

Driving into Leadville, I'm so overcome by emotion at the sight of the mountains, I have to pull over on the shoulder. To the west rises the broad summit of Mount Elbert, at 14,440 feet, the highest peak in Colorado. The Leadville 100 course snakes along the mountain's broad, forested base to Twin Lakes, then climbs steeply to Hope Pass and down the other side to Winfield. I've run it in my body, and now, as I blink back tears of gratitude, for being here and being healed—finally whole—I'm running it in my mind.

"Do not doubt that green mountains are always walking," Dogen wrote. Even something so stalwart as a mountain, seemingly so still, is dynamic and alive. Whatever happens—good, bad, ugly, finish or drop—will be icing on the cake, a celebration of how I've gotten here and what I've learned, the least of which is about running: Make sincere effort for the good. Be yourself. Let go. Keep going.

There are a million things to do before the starting gun goes off. Read, write, pack my drop bags full of supplies, eat. Eat a lot. Sit. Run only a little. Ride my bike around town. Eat some more. In the cafe in town, I run into Tim and his crew from Kentucky. He agrees to lend me his friend and pacer, Joe, to run with me for sixteen miles at mile sixty-two. "This is the woman who's going to win Leadville," Tim brags to the waitress. I can feel my face redden and I elbow him, pretending to laugh it off. On his paper placemat he draws a crayon picture of a woman running along a mountain top, her brown ponytail swinging in the air. "Tape it to the wall," he tells the waitress. "You'll see."

On the way home, I pass a small, gabled Victorian. It's similar to all the other old mining-era houses in town, though much more derelict. It has lavender curlicue trim with peeling paint and a scalloped detail above the front door that has seen better days. Behind a chain-link fence, a faded whitewater kayak lies beached in the weedy yard. The front door looks fused shut, as though it hasn't been opened in years. Painted directly on the glass panes is a weathered sign that reads LEADVILLE COSMOLOGY MUSEUM. And below that, in letters so sun-faded I have to look twice, DIVINE SPIRIT OVER MATTER.

In less than forty-eight hours I'll join more than 700 runners on the starting line. Fewer than half of us will finish. I decide I'm going to love myself for simply getting here, which has not been so simple. All those low days of doubt in the early spring, waking with a log on my heart, lying in the dirt, wondering if I could run home. All the days before that, days of brokenness, injury, fear. And the wondrous days, too: floating above the wooded trails at the lake in Canada, jumping in the water with all my clothes on, the sharp California rain pelting down so long ago, two dusty Advil in the dirt at the bottom of the Grand Canyon.

I remember riding my bike one-legged, imagining what it would feel like to run one hundred miles through the mountains: *miso soup in the middle of the night, meadows blazing with wildflowers.*

Running or racing, it doesn't matter. It's always about the feeling.

—

Friday night, after all the details are done and my alarm set for 3:00 a.m., I pull out my notebook.

> *Going to bed peaceful. Feeling ready. All roads lead here.*
> *This is my time and place. I can do it. I will do it and it will*
> *be beautiful. This is my time.*

What seems like one minute later, I wake in the dark, slip out of bed. In the dim light of the kitchen, I force-feed myself two bowls of instant oatmeal and write two words in black Sharpie on the back of my left hand: SMILE and FLOW. I want to move with the mountains and to remember the joy I feel when I run—the true reason I run.

At the starting line it is nowhere close to morning. The pavement is wet, the air damp and cold. I hug Steve and my friend Susie, smiling through tears. Already I've done it. Getting here was the hardest part.

I can tell you what happened next. I stood shoulder to shoulder with runners in the front of the corral; the race director, Ken, fired the gun; and I ran into the still-black night. Spectators lined the road out of town, a man in a white bathrobe stood in the cone of his porch light, waving to us. "Only 99.5 miles to go!" he shouted. We cheered our approval.

Off the road and into the forest, around Turquoise Lake in the dark before dawn, I use the runners in front of me to keep my pace in check. Shoe soles slapping dirt and rocks, soft conversations rising around me, the rhythm of the day, and my own rhythm, building in me. At first light, a guy with a John Denver bob and a jiggly fanny pack straight out of the 1980s spontaneously screams *Lead-FUCKING-ville!* into the forest, and I scream it back, an involuntary rallying cry and pure glee rolled into one.

I have no idea where I am in the pack, on purpose. My brother-in-law's friend Wes, an experienced mountain ultra runner who offered to pace me the last twenty-five miles to the finish told me, "Don't even think about racing this thing until mile sixty-three."

Climbing Sugarloaf, a photographer crouches in the grass with his camera. "Second woman!" he calls as I pass.

Oh NOOOO, I think. *It's too soon.*

And then, *This changes nothing. Smile and flow.*

The top of the mountain comes into view. How lovely it is. There is nothing to worry about. The mountains are alive, and I am moving with them. "Flow with the river of time," I tell myself out loud as I crest the summit.

—

A long race is like all of life lived in a single day.

It rained and the sun came out. I ate energy gels and drank Coke and climbed Hope Pass going south and then back up again going north, this time with Steve pacing me. We passed dozens of runners charging downhill, and one cried out "Great job!" in an Australian accent. Steve, behind me, erupts into song. *I come from the land down under!* Over and over we belt out Men at Work songs, until at last we ascend out of the trees and into the alpine and reach the top of Hope Pass at 12,600 feet. Steve hands me a Styrofoam cup of miso soup at the aid station, then it's nowhere to go but down.

In Twin Lakes, I catch up with the first-place woman—her name is Addie, Steve tells me—and Steve hands me over to Joe, and together he and I work our way up the long hill and into the lead.

We're at mile sixty-three.

I have the odd sensation of being neither ahead of nor behind myself, but right where I am, exactly in the center of effort—not more than I can handle, not less. Just right. Running as running, as the mountain itself.

Am I tired? If so, I can't feel it. I'm eating constantly, whatever looks good on the aid station tables, and energy gels that Joe offers me precisely every thirty minutes. The trail curves and winds along the base of the mountains. We are on a trail, then a dirt road. "Do you want some music?" Joe asks, "because I've got some Gordon Lightfoot on my phone." I'm about to laugh at what obviously must be a joke—who under the age of eighty listens to Gordon Lightfoot?!—but I can tell from his earnest tone that he's serious and I feel like hugging him.

Instead, I cue Whitesnake's "Here I Go Again" and turn it up to ten.

Here I go again on my own
Goin' down the only road I've ever known.

The sun sets and I draft behind Joe in a stiff headwind coming into mile seventy-five and there are my friends and my daughters, now wearing disco costumes, and Steve is off fly-fishing, but in his place is a guy with a huge grin whom I've never seen before. It's Wes. He's going to run home with me.

"There are two things I'm not going to tell you," Wes says once we're underway. His pack is massive, made for mountaineering—he must have brought gear for every possible survival scenario. "But there's one thing I will tell you: Addie ran a 100k race a month ago and she's tired."

We're keeping a good pace along a paved road to the base of the last big climb. Wes's secret weapon is information management. He is very composed, running behind me while surreptitiously texting my brother-in-law, Neal, who's manning the race splits online from his house in California. We've got twenty minutes on Addie.

Our gap may be widening, but I don't spend a second thinking about it. We hike as fast as we can, through five false summits and deepening twilight, to the top of Sugarloaf, where my eyes go fuzzy and I feel the first edges of panic emerging. "Wes!" I shout, though he's right on my heels. "I'm having trouble seeing! I think I'm going blind!" I've heard about this: ultra runners temporarily losing their sight from dust in their corneas.

Wes says calmly, "Turn on your headlamp, Katie."

I flick on my light. The world, in focus, reveals sharp edges of pine trees. Someone has hung twinkly solar lights from the boughs.

It's chilly and starting to drizzle. We're eighteen miles—and at least three hours—from the finish. "Wes!" I whimper. "Should I put on my jacket?"

He says, "As long as we keep moving, you shouldn't need it."

We keep moving.

Turquoise Lake is a blurred outline against the darkness. At the aid station, Steve is back but the girls are gone, back at the rental house, sleeping. Slurp some soup, keep moving, thirteen miles to go. Wes, working the cell phone, reports Addie is now thirty minutes back.

My heart jumps to my throat. *Calm down. Anything can happen.* Wes and I run alongside the lake, silent for what feels like miles but may only be minutes. I try to focus on picking up my feet so my shoes don't snag on rocks. One step at a time is the only way I'll get there.

After a while Wes says quietly, "Addie would have to have a complete turnaround and at the same time you would have to have a total disaster for you not to win at this point."

For the first time all day, I allow myself to think about winning, to feel it. My heart backflips and a tiny cog clicks inside my mind—an idea. "What time is it?" I ask Wes. My watch battery died hours ago, and I have no concept of time, except that it's dark. It could be one in the morning for all I know.

"Not quite ten."

My brain is muddled, but I can still manage rudimentary math. I have less than twelve miles to go. If I can keep this pace, roughly ten-minute miles, I will finish before midnight. In under twenty hours. In all my last-minute calculations, I never once pictured this.

"Do you think I can go sub-twenty? Should we try?" I ask Wes, already knowing I will—not for success or validation, but to go all the way, to give everything: total, continuous effort, right up to the very end.

I can tell Wes is smiling when he answers, "Yes," as though the word has been in his mouth all night, just waiting to come out. "But let's be conservative until we get off the trail and onto the dirt road."

We pass the boat ramp and campsites, where people in tents stick their heads out to cheer for us, and leave the trail near the dam and veer up onto a road. Soon there is an aid station, volunteers in headlamps huddled around tables, calling me by name. I'm smiling so hard my face hurts, though maybe I dream it because we pass through quickly, not pushing toward the finish as much as being pulled by it.

Now we can see the lights of Leadville reflecting off the clouds. It is damp and sort of drizzling and quite chilly, but I have long stopped thinking. I'm just moving, I am movement. The return to town is a long gradual uphill on dirt roads, I remember it from the way out when I was holding back my speed. Now I am trying to maintain it. Behind me, Wes has gone very quiet, and I take his silence to mean we've slipped off our pace. Then I think of what he said a few miles back. "No matter happens, when you have hard days, don't forget, you will always be a Leadville champion."

No matter what happens.

The first streetlight on the edge of town emits a feeble glow. "So it's after midnight, right?" I ask, dejection creeping into my voice. I hear Wes fumbling with his jacket. A long pause. Then, "No, it's 11:49."

I'm speechless, but my legs are supersonic. We veer onto Sixth and run side by side up the long, gradual hill where I'd been six weeks before, narrating then what is unfolding now. *They said it couldn't be dooone!*

No matter what happens.

Ahead. Down a hill. The finish chute, lights, friends, family, everything, the whole of life. Legs wheeling. Steve is a stilted shadow on the side of the road a hundred feet before the finish line, waiting for me. Steve! He holds out his hands, he is yelling my name, I put my hands on his and then keep going, flying now.

Above the finish line, a shooting star streaks through a small hole in the clouds, a brief flash in the dark, just the narrowest of openings in the black, wet sky. "Wes!" I cry. "Did you see that?"

"Yes!" His voice fainter now, behind me, choked with emotion. "Someone up there is looking out for you!"

I am running for the tape and then I am breaking it, running into the outstretched arms of my girls, my friends, bringing everything above me, around me, behind me, ahead of me, with me.

27. CONTINUOUS MISTAKE

Later, much later, in the middle of the next night, I lay in bed. I couldn't tell where my legs ended and the bed began. I couldn't tell if I was upside down or not, if my head faced the foot of the bed, if my feet had crawled halfway up the wall. If I was alone, if the voices I heard were inside my head or outside of it. All of the above were at one point true. I was sleeping but not sleeping. Through the window, I could hear people walking along the road, talking loudly, shouting, possibly drunk. There was always someone drunk and hollering after midnight in Leadville. Streetlights shone through the window's gauzy curtain.

In the morning, I woke, and nothing seemed like a dream. My legs had concretized. Time had taken on strange, amorphous proportions, and my phone beeped incessantly. CONGRATULATIONS ON YOUR SUCCESS, wrote my stepfather. I blinked, read his text again, and sent my own. THANK YOU.

My mind flashed to the race—the feeling of flying through the dark, papery moth wings beating in my chest. The feeling of coming home. I couldn't believe what I'd done, what had happened.

But, truthfully, I could. I really could.

—

I hadn't set out to win Leadville. I'd simply stuck with my plan: to stay in flow for as long as I could and then hold on till the end. I'd eaten all my calories. I'd used my trekking poles and sang Men at Work and loved my husband the whole way up Hope Pass. I ran a block along a dirt road through Twin Lakes beside Maisy, who was dressed as a Whoopie cushion, and high-fived strangers cheering my name and old friends and others I'd just met but felt as though I'd known forever. I drafted behind Joe and listened to Whitesnake and worried when Wes grew quiet. I ran through a river in sopping sneakers and watched the sun set and rode the mountains all the way to the end.

In the damp dark at the finish line, I had turned to Wes. "What were the two things you didn't want to tell me?"

He grinned. "That Addie is a 2:30 marathoner. And that this morning, I ran the Pikes Peak Ascent."

I burst out laughing. I'd been sure that Wes's silence meant I was moving too slowly, but really he was just tired from running his own race up a 14,000-foot mountain, silly Wes! I hugged him hard, giddy with relief. Thank God I hadn't known how fast Addie was!

None of this, though, accounts for what really happened.

Flow with the river of time, I'd told myself. And I did, for one hundred miles and nearly twenty hours, and the more I smiled, the more I flowed, and the more I flowed, the more I smiled, until at the very last second a star shot through the black night—a kind of magic, here and then gone.

"It is necessary for us to encourage ourselves and to make an effort up to the last moment, when all effort disappears," Suzuki Roshi had written in *Zen Mind, Beginner's Mind*.

I felt as though I'd been floating all day and could just keep going and going—like time itself. For a little while at least, I'd closed the gap. It wasn't beginner's luck that had helped me win Leadville, it was beginner's mind.

—

A few days after I got home, I got a card in the mail from an acquaintance. "In the tradition of the Tarahamara and the Japanese monks, you are a true spirit runner!" she wrote. "Thank you for reminding us what is possible when our human selves meet our divine selves." What had happened in Leadville seemed indescribable—*divine spirit over matter*—but she understood.

That evening I went to a talk at the Zen center. Natalie and I walked up the dirt road together. My feet were still swollen from the race, bloated and flayed like dead fish, but I was peaceful, more peaceful than I could ever remember, wholly different and yet more myself than I'd ever been.

I told Natalie everything. "It was your time," she said. "When there's no gap, all of life gets behind you," Natalie went on, "the trees and the dirt and the mountains and people. Everything." Kr used to tell her this. All the parts of my life—writing and mothering, running and Zen—had converged in Leadville. I'd tapped into something bigger than myself and had ridden it to an outcome I never could have imagined. Like Zen, it defied analysis or interpretation. I couldn't understand it with my brain. I had to touch it with another part of myself.

Upaya's head priest, Roshi Joan Halifax, spoke that evening about "continuous mistake"—a phrase sometimes used to describe Zen practice. Like continuous effort, it refers to the things we do over and over, sometimes botching them, other times succeeding, but always learning and growing into. She said this with kindness and gentle exasperation, like *When will we* ever *learn?* Maybe never. Welcome to being alive.

It was like the Buddhist vow to save all sentient beings from suffering by ferrying them across a river in a raft. I loved the rafting metaphor because of how utterly impossible it was. It would take lifetime after lifetime and still you could never ever do it, you could never get every single being to the other side. But to keep practicing without concern for your guaranteed failure is in its own way a triumph. By trying and falling short, you are in fact succeeding. There's no distance between the two.

I was trying but failing to sit cross-legged on the zafu. My fish feet stuck out in front of me, too flabby to fold. I had just run a hundred miles, surpassed limits I thought unsurpassable, but all around me people were sitting with stoic blank faces like it was any old Wednesday, a routine night in this routine life. So many scenes flashed before me. The river, flipping the raft, falling. Should I have fallen more easily? Should I have run less? Should I have forgiven Steve sooner? *It's all my fault.* I mouthed words to myself. They felt thick on my tongue, wrong, like the meaty fish that clung to my ankles. But also, strangely liberating. To embrace it all, equally, is to let it go.

"We are big enough to absorb blame," Roshi Joan went on. "Eat the blame, eat your ego, it will make you strong."

If I held it lightly in my mind, I could almost see how it worked. Eating failure is different than wallowing in shame. It's releasing shame. I thought of the shame I carried and of the fury beneath the shame, of the shame and fury we all carry. Dropping it, we become lighter, more nimble. Unburdened, we have the stamina and ease to keep trying and keep failing and the fortitude to know that failing won't stop us from trying and succeeding—over and over.

It reminded me of a line in *Zen Mind*. "If you continue this practice every day, you will obtain a wonderful power. Before you obtain it, it is something wonderful, but after you obtain it, it is nothing special. It is just you yourself."

I knew that running and wildness and writing were my continuous mistakes, the ones I would keep making again and again, in some way or another, the way we all do, because we are dumb animals and also, mostly, because we are hopeful and good, and we will always keep going.

—

The sun is still high in the sky when the talk lets out and we file quietly into the late summer evening. Four months from now, on a dark snowy night, I will give my own talk, but I don't know this yet. What I know is that the sunflowers have just started to bloom along the roadside and the gravel crunches beneath my feet as I walk slowly back to my car. A woman comes up behind me. "Are you Katie?" she asks? "The runner?"

I nod, "Yes," I say.

"You are incredible."

"Thank you," I say, meaning it truly.

Watching her walk away, I want to add but don't, *I'm sorry.*

—

On another day less than a year later, I will be running along on the same trail where Steve and I forgave each other when my mind wanders, as it often does, back to Leadville. Winning had changed everything and nothing. The phone rang and didn't ring. I kept running. My book about my father came out. The phone rang and didn't ring. I kept writing. Some days felt like soaring and others like slogging.

Races would be won and lost—though no race is ever really lost—and I'd keep getting blown off course, like we all do. And all the while, I'd have to keep forgetting what I'd done while also never, as Wes had counseled me, forgetting.

The willows along the creek are brushy and green, aromatic in the spring morning air. Loving Steve will always smell like this: willows after a heavy dew, their sweet, damp feet rooting fast to the earth. Like rivers and hope. I wonder suddenly if Steve has tasted the shame of coming up short. If he knows what it's like to fail and fall. In between one footfall and the next, I realize. *Oh, yes*.

Flipping the raft on the Middle Fork must have felt that way to him.

Only I hadn't loved him fully through it. I'd blamed him and been angry. How awful that must have been for him, compounding his regret. Steve had always loved me in his way, even though it wasn't always my way. Love, too, is our continuous mistake.

—

For now, though, it's still that August evening, the crickets singing through the open window. Steve's reading on the couch when I get home from the Dharma talk. I barely have a chance to say hello before he starts in: "So this moth walks into a podiatrist's office. 'I'm having trouble with my marriage,' the moth tells the doctor. 'I don't like my job and am feeling unfulfilled at home. I realize I am going to die. I think I'm having an existential crisis.'"

"Wait," I interrupt. "Do moths have feet?"

Steve rolls his eyes, faking impatience. "No." Pauses, then: "So, the podiatrist looks at the moth and says, 'It sounds like you need a psychiatrist. I am a podiatrist. Why did you come to me?'" A glimmer of a smile creeps across Steve's face; I force a blank, expectant look, but inside I'm already crying with laughter. "'Because the light was on,' the moth said."

I know where Steve's humor comes from. It comes from the middle of his life. Even when he snaps at me to move my Leadville trophy, a miniature rusted iron mining cart that's been spilling crumbly rocks all over the dining room table for weeks, even in his short-temperedness, he's in the middle of his life. Just as I'm in the middle of mine. And we're in the middle of ours, together: love, conflict, laughter—all of it always entwined.

Outside, through the open window, the coyotes are howling and yipping. They are very loud and close. We've seen their dens, holes hollowed into the sandy dirt behind our house. They're in the middle of their lives, too.

We all hold within us the desire to make something real and to *be* real. Yes, you exist, you are seen, your feet are planted on this earth, and you move through it. You are not a figment of your own storytelling or imagination. You are here, and by the simple fact of being here, in the middle of your life, you will make one beautiful mistake after another, a steady stream of failures, rising and falling and rising again—proof that you are human and alive, open to all possibilities, knowing and being known without knowing anything at all.

It's just like Georgia O'Keeffe's painting *Anything*. Anything is possible when you live like this. And also, everything.

28. SOMETIMES A FLASHING

There are entire books devoted to enlightenment stories, koans stretching back through the ages. Some are sublime, others so mundane as to seem completely ridiculous, deep truths wrapped in absurdities, like the punchline of a joke or a *Saturday Night Live* skit. An ancient monk stubs his toe on a gate and is awakened; another, sweeping the yard, hears a pebble strike a piece of bamboo; some get their fingers or other appendages chopped off by their masters; others, like Dogen, hear a turning word from their teachers and all of reality cracks open.

Awakening can happen anywhere—on trains, on mountaintops, in cold dark monasteries before dawn, 1,200 years ago and this very morning. You would not believe the stories! Are they myth or fact, legend or truth? Don't worry about it too much.

My favorites are the ones about regular people doing everyday things when all at once they're overcome by the totality of existence and at the same time its utter transience. Life and death in an instant! Nothing separates the two, not even a hair's breadth of difference. "Each moment, all beings, is this entire world," Dogen wrote. "Reflect if any being or any world is left out of the present."

Life is a series of flickerings, like lightning bugs pulsing in a meadow or streetlamps blinking randomly in the blackness. Tiny items of astonishment on the tick list of existence. At first glance they might not look like much. Look again.

These sudden flashings, shot up like flares in the night, came and went and left me changed but also the same. I was still my semi-neurotic self, sort of disheveled, maybe a smidge more settled, a little less prone to terror, not quite so fixated on having answers or really any clue at all. The world would always keep us guessing, there was no way around it, and going down the mountain was just as hard as going up. No matter how dazzling your epiphany at the top, how stupendous the view, you still have to reenter your life.

I'd stopped trying to hold onto the flashings. I knew they'd come again, had been coming all along. "The sky is never surprised when all of a sudden a thunderbolt breaks through," Suzuki Roshi had written. "And when the lightning does flash, a wonderful sight may be seen. When we have emptiness we are always prepared for watching the flashing."

Zen is energy arising. Always, everywhere. It really is that simple. "Ordinary mind is the way," goes the famous koan. "If you try to turn toward it, you go against it." You can practice diligently and with great purpose, but you can't try to get enlightened. In the words of Katagiri Roshi, "Finally, all you have to do is just live."

—

If I were to tell you the story of my weirdest awakening so far, it would go like this: I was stopped at a red light, listening to Eddie Money.

It's the spring before the pandemic. I'm still racing, still filling notebooks. The girls are growing, the job description is changing. Physically, motherhood has stopped kicking my ass. It's a mental game now.

I'm in the car. The radio's on, the way it almost always is when I drive, and I'm flipping mindlessly through the stations to avoid commercials and get to the good songs. Any song with a story is a good song. I ease up to the light at East Alameda. Big 98.5 Albuquerque's Greatest Hits is playing "Take Me Home Tonight." My window's open and I know all the words and I sing without thinking. *Take me home tonight I don't wanna let you go til you see the light.* The traffic light turns red. Pedestrians are crossing in the crosswalk, and the sun is out after two days of clouds and rain. I'm running late, as usual, but I'm not in a rush, I'm just belting out

> *I get frightened in all this darkness*
> *I get nightmares, I hate to sleep alone.*

All the world is in this moment, with Eddie Money singing and me singing along with Eddie Money. It hits me that I've never understood the chorus. *It's just like Ronnie says . . . just like Ronnie sa-aaays.* Who in the hell is Ronnie? I realize I have no idea. I've sung it this way forever because we used to call my stepbrother Ronnie when he was a kid, but the lyrics may in fact have nothing to do with Ronnie, never have had anything to do with Ronnie. Maybe he's not even saying Ronnie. It doesn't matter. The world is alive and I'm in it, feeling its aliveness and mine at the same time. Everything is enough and exactly as it should be, in my car at the red light at East Alameda and Paseo de Peralta on an April morning in Santa Fe, while I tap my fingers to the beat on the steering wheel, completely here, still wishing for the world to slow down just a little, but not urgently, simply seeing clearly that this is one moment, the only moment, and I am in it.

The light changes and I ease through a left turn, still singing out loud, and then the song ends, and I change the station, and the moment is over.

What did I know differently after that? I can't tell you anything but this: the thing Dogen said about time is true. All moments are included in this very moment. Stretch out your arms as wide as they can go, the way I'm doing now. Can you see me? It's this big, the whole of everything, expanding.

And also this small.

29. CLEAR WATER

You can't see the end until you're almost upon it.

The place where the two rivers meet is camouflaged by the canyon. The canyon twists against itself, the river threading through the middle, pushing against the walls. You can almost feel it happening, the force of water bending the world to its will. In places the canyon is pinched and tight, the river tumbling over boulders, wending brightly below the sky. Sometimes the cleft in the canyon is so narrow you cannot tell which way it turns, if it is a bend in the river, or the end of the river.

Your eyes have become accustomed to reading the walls in front of you, straining for clues of what's to come, but even so, the canyon is a mirage. It guards its secrets closely. Does the river go left or right? You are too far away to tell, or sometimes too near. Your eyes see what your mind wants them to—you do not want the river to end, but also you do.

The river does not end, of course. No river does. It joins another and continues flowing.

—

We went back to the Middle Fork. It was the first summer of the pandemic and our annual trip to Canada was canceled, the border closed indefinitely. We drove north to Sun Valley, sixteen hours.

Everything felt different. The girls were ten and twelve, old enough to come along. The summer I didn't die was so far away; I'd finally read the Jim Harrison book, and it was nothing like my story after all. I'd released it. "If you seek for freedom, you cannot find it," Suzuki Roshi writes in *Zen Mind*. "Our way is not always to go in one direction. Sometimes we go east; sometimes we go west." Change is the only true constant. We were all so different now.

We'd signed up for a guided trip. There were twenty other guests. Pippa and Maisy fought over who got to sit with the cool, young twenty-something artist and her Hollywood actor boyfriend who took them under their wing. The most senior guide, Buzz, in his early seventies, taught them card tricks. The river was lapis and clear, the color of the sky, the rapids lower and slower in July than they'd been that June, a river lazing into midsummer. Fleabane, gooseberry, lupine burst forth along the shore. Steve fished for cutthroats till dark. My notebook was fir green, smudged with dirt. It was our fourteenth wedding anniversary.

Each afternoon when we got to camp, I went for a run along the river trail. It was rocky and faint in places, sometimes hugging the edge of choppy talus slopes that dropped steeply to the river. It was a long way to fall. I ran slowly, carefully, matching my pace to the trail.

The running was not what I expected. The trail was rougher, overgrown, not so straightforward. You had to watch your footing, you could not run free. In Zen you are supposed to get rid of everything extra from your practice and just do the thing itself, completely. The river had its own flow. Maybe the running was extra.

One day, as I ran upstream from camp, a raven swooped down and attacked me from behind, scrabbling my scalp with its sharp talons. I screamed and started sprinting, half alarmed, half laughing as the bird chased me maniacally for a quarter mile, flapping from tree to tree, fixing me with its devilish black eyes. In all my years outside, this was a new one.

Back in camp, it was cocktail hour, and the Idaho old-timers—because of course there were Idaho old-timers—were drinking red wine in plastic cups, gabbing with their friends in camp chairs at the water's edge. I tell Pippa and Maisy, as I so often do, that they must promise to row me downstream through a wilderness canyon when I'm eighty. "Of course we will, Mama," they say, laughing like children because they are.

The raven smacked Steve as well, while he was fly-fishing. Of all the others in camp, the bird found Steve. We decided it must have been our sunglasses pushed up on our heads; the shiny, reflective lenses lured the bird. Or the fact that each of us had been alone. Or maybe the raven just had a very good sense of humor. Either way, we laughed for a long time about that raven. We were going to get a lot of years out of that bird.

—

But it was the water that moved me the most. Its clarity and brightness, the enlivening briskness when we jumped off a downed, bark-skinned tree into the river. The current was strong, unending, with stern eddy lines that you had to work to get through and rapids stirring the surface into glittery white waves. "Pool and drop," Steve proudly reminded me—long, busy sections of whitewater followed by still water. The pools were so transparent they reminded me of a line from one of Dogen's poems, "clear water all the way to the bottom," brown cobbles whizzing past, each one nestled upon another like an intricate, ever-changing puzzle. The stones were not moving, we were.

The rock we'd hit had a name. It was called Doors Rock, one of the guides told me on the first day. How appropriate, I thought. An opening into a life I hadn't wanted to enter but that had led me out, as doors do, to the other side. And now here we were again. The rock was coming up fast, and I gripped my paddle with one hand and the raft with the other and tried to breathe, until there it was. It looked just like the mean, gray pyramidal rock in my memory, waiting to grab you. It was not nothing, and in a way I was glad to see it. "It doesn't look too bad, but it's weird, it sucks a raft in the wrong way," our guide said. "It doesn't behave like the other rocks in the river." We were going to clear it by three boats' lengths. It was coming and then it was going, we were past it.

It sailed by, upstream of us, and with it, the last four years—in some ways the best I'd known, but also the hardest.

This was life, I guess. Our wild, dirty life.

—

On the last night, Steve and I stretch our sleeping bag on a tarp under the star-frazzled sky and lie side by side on our backs. We're looking for a comet called Neowise. The next time it will be visible with the naked eye will be in 7,000 years.

"We'll be so old by then," I say to Steve, feeling for his hand in the dark.

I can't see his smile, but I can hear it. "Old as fuck," he agrees.

In the morning, the Idaho old-timers pay Maisy ten dollars apiece to carry their gear bags down to the rafts. Eighty-year-old Keith tips her an extra five. She'll make a good guide someday.

I want to live on rivers, but I can't. *We* can't. We round the last bend and the canyon releases us, across the murky stripe in the river and into the Main Salmon's wide channel. On the far bank I can see the wooden sign that points back upstream into the Middle Fork's Impassable Canyon, the direction from which we've come: "Yonder lies the Idaho Wilderness."

I think about this trip and our first Middle Fork trip, by some accounts a spectacular disaster. I had been so sure this one would be better, but you couldn't say that. No, not necessarily. Not better, not worse, not good, not bad.

It was just itself.

It was the bald eagle posing regally in a dead ponderosa, the tree's bark blackened and puffy like a scorched marshmallow, the scars of a forest burned down to cinders. The maniacal raven, a rowdy game of capture the flag with the California crew in a meadow at dusk. Heart-shaped rocks on the first morning's beach.

"There are so many!" I'd exclaimed to Steve as I bent down to pick up a stone.

"There are if you're looking," he said, nodding. "There are if you're looking."

It was all of us, together, and the river and the mountains. "Above all waters are mountains," Dogen had written. You can't always see the mountains when you're in the canyon, but you know they're there, snow clinging to north-facing couloirs, jagged tops shearing the sky. High over the hump of the divide, far out of sight, are more mountains and more canyons, running deep with their own rivers, rivers feeding the mountains and the mountains making rivers.

"One thing flows into another and cannot be grasped," Suzuki Roshi wrote at the end of *Zen Mind*.

Mountains teach us how to get up, and rivers how to fall. But now I see there's no difference. Mountains and rivers, courage and fear, winning and losing, holding on and letting go—they're the same thing after all.

How do you tell a story that's beyond words? You start where you are.

Now, on a lake, in summer. The wind is up, the sailboats across the bay plow headlong through pewter waves. A storm is coming; I can see the veil of rain to the north. It's any day in any summer, but also it is exactly now. Just as, by the time you read this, it will be then.

I pull a notebook from my shelf, flip at random to a page. It's a game I play sometimes. What will I find, where will it take me? I remember the bright April quarantine morning—the deep blue sky and so much silence. I am riding my bicycle fast through a park when I see a Tibetan monk coming out of a Porta-Potty. His long saffron robes swish the ground. He sees me see him, and the sadness I feel as our eyes meet equals my gladness.

We are cocooned in our separate worlds, yet we pass and somehow touch each other. Our moments touch.

My notebooks are a map of the mountains. They trace the topography of rivers, the coordinates of loneliness and love. Reading them again, I finally understand the classic koan, "Is the flag blowing or the wind?" Neither, the koan tells us. Just as it was never merely the mountains moving, nor the waters, nor, even, my body. More than anything, it was my mind.

Outside, the air is gray and still; the lake has surrendered to an exquisite, temporary calm. For an instant, everything seems to stand still. The story that started with a talk on a snowy night has caught up to itself, or I have caught up to it. But like the clouds storming toward us and past us, our stories don't stop. They just keep going.

I know nothing of what lies ahead. No one does. We only think we do. Occasionally something dazzling will fork the dark sky, and someone somewhere will be there to see it.

All these years, I've been out collecting, foraging for flashes, bursts of everyday brilliance that fall by chance from a shelf, out of the sky, into my open hands, so that some day—this one—I could give them to you.

ACKNOWLEDGMENTS

Much of this book was written on traditional Puebloan lands of the Tewa people, O'gah'poh geh Owingeh (White Shell Water Place), or Santa Fe, New Mexico. I extend deep gratitude and respect for the ancestors who came before and the stewards who continue to care for this land today.

I am infinitely grateful to Steve, Pippa, and Maisy for their unwavering love and support, good humor, and perspective.

Thank you to my family and my many friends for their kindness and laughter. Especially to my mother and stepfather, for a boat-house in which to write parts of this book.

Honorable mention goes to Kate Ferlic, for her sharp eyes and legal expertise, for letting me in on the best lunch order at The Shed (ground beef enchiladas, flat; extra red chile, burnt; egg over medium), and for always asking the right questions.

Thank you, my Leadville family and crew: Wes, Erika, Blair, Steve, Susie (brave over perfect!), Joe, Tim, Ken, and Merilee, as well as assorted, semi-feral children in costumes.

Thank you to Resolana Farms, for providing unfettered space and time to write.

Deep bow of gratitude to my mentors and teachers, and to their teachers before them, including Natalie Goldberg, Henry Shukman, Norman Fischer, Matthew Palevsky, and Noah Rossetter. Special gratitude to Roshi Joan Halifax for inviting me to speak at Upaya Zen Center in December 2018; that talk became the bones of this book.

I would be remiss if I didn't also thank my surgeon, for keeping his word and doing his very best to give me a bionic knee.

To my wonderful literary agent, Danielle Svetcov, thank you for always seeing the wildness in this story and reminding me to believe.

To my my writer and editor friends—Marin Sardy, Julia Goldberg, Will Palmer—and to one of my earliest readers, Laura Deykerhoff: thank you for your encouragement and sound advice.

Thank you to my editor, Miranda Perrone, for her deep and mindful dedication to this story; to Katie Eberle for a brilliant cover that so beautifully expresses the feeling of this book; to Liz McKellar, Katie Sheehan, Jess Brown, and Sarah Arriagada, and to all those at Parallax Press who helped to bring this book into being. Thank you also to Jacob Surpin, for seeing this story from the start, and to Jake MacPhail, for your thoughtful copyediting. It's an honor be part of Thich Nhat Hanh's publishing vision.

And, always, to the land and water—mountains and rivers, deserts, forests, canyons, and lakes: true spirit teachers.

And to you, my readers, thank you.

SOURCES

Heartfelt recognition and respect to these teachers and texts whose words proved instructive and instrumental in the writing of this book. If you are interested in these titles and teachings, please inquire about them at your local independent bookstore. Thank you.

Suzuki, Shunryū. *Zen Mind Beginner's Mind: Informal Talks on Zen Meditation and Practice*. Boulder: Shambhala, 2011.

Tanahashi, Kazuaki, ed. *Moon in a Dewdrop: Writings of Zen Master Dōgen*. San Francisco: North Point Press, 1995.

Katagiri, Dainin. *Each Moment Is the Universe: Zen and the Way of Being Time*. Edited by Andrea Martin. Boulder: Shambhala, 2007.

Katagiri, Dainin. *The Light that Shines Through Infinity: Zen and the Energy of Life*. Edited by Andrea Martin. Boulder: Shambhala, 2017.

Katagiri, Dainin, *Returning to Silence: Zen Practice in Daily Life*. Edited by Yūko Conniff and Willa Hathaway. Boulder: Shambhala, 1988.

An audio archive of Dainin Katagiri's Dharma talks are available online on the Minnesota Zen Center website: *https://www.mnzencenter.org/the-dainin-katagiri-audio-archive*.

ABOUT THE AUTHOR

Katie Arnold is the author of *Running Home* and a longtime contributor to *Outside* magazine. A Zen practitioner and elite ultra runner, Katie teaches writing workshop and running retreats exploring the link between movement and creativity. Her writing has been featured in *The New York Times, The Wall Street Journal. ESPN The Magazine, Runner's World,* and *Elle, among others,* as well as on *NPR Weekend Edition Sunday* and *The Upaya Zen Center Podcast.* She has been awarded creative fellowships from MacDowell and Ucross. Katie lives in Santa Fe, New Mexico, with her husband, Steve Barrett, their two daughters, and two dogs.